Journey Into the Mythic DEEP

Journey Into the Mythic DEEP

Seven Above Seven Below

(Enhanced Screenplay)

Based on Cougar's other works:

Angels in the Light,

Antahkarana:

The Light Web Of Life

&

Wisdom of the

Ancient EL-ders

Robert Cougar Penhaligon

Graphic Assistant C.G. Dahlin

Copyright © August 2022 Robert Cougar Penhaligon

IngramSpark Indie Pub.

No portion of this book may be reproduced by any means without prior written permission by the author, except in the case of brief quotations.

All rights reserved.
ISBN-13: 9798218005405

Genres:
1. NDE
2. Consciousness
3. Immortality
4. Angels
5. Human Potential
6. Moral Philosophy
7. Mythology

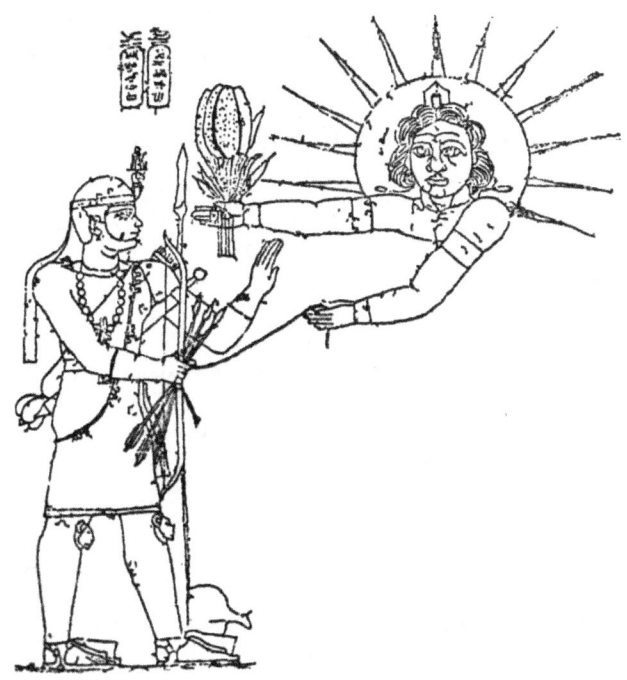

Radiant El blesses Kosh
Circa 2000 B.C.

"Cougar's NDEs (experiences with death)
are phenomenal and well written. He seems
to be an anointed person."
- Mike Ilitch, Jr., producer of *Angriest Man in Brooklyn 2014,
Stuck in Love 2012, Lost in Space 1998.*

"Cougar probably has had the most important series of NDEs of
any human being alive today. He has a major role to play in the
future of our planet. His incredible life is an inspiration to me."
- Patrick Wells, producer of *At Jesus' Side (Roma Downey) 2008,
I Love You To Death 1990, Honor Bound 1988, Young Blood 1986.*

"Your experiences have been some of the
most profound I have ever heard."
- Bruce Greyson, MD., Professor Emeritus of Psychiatry
& Neurobehavioral Sciences. Most active NDE researcher.
Author of *After (Death & Beyond) 2021.*

"Out of the thousands on my website, Cougar's 3rd NDE alone,
I consider in the top 5 NDEs I have ever read. The parallels to
Ancient Sumerian texts of the
Goddess Inanna are amazing."
- Jody Long, attorney and webmaster of NDERF
(largest NDE website in the world), author of
*God's Fingerprints, Impressions of NDEs
and From Soul To Soulmate.*

"Several Enlightening experiences came through
for me. I believe that all readers will be touched
at some level."
- Marajen Moore, Seed Center publisher of
The Lazy Man's Guide to Enlightenment 1972.

"A remarkable screenplay. Vivid and engaging
with a universal message."
- Jeffery Long, MD., NDE researcher,
author of *Evidence of the Afterlife 2010
and God in the Afterlife 2016.*

It was a dark and stormy night...

No moon is in sight.

Lost in the middle of the ocean.

Lightning flashes.

Waves are seen and heard in thunderous rolls.

The mystery and power of THE DEEP is felt.

Another flash!

An ancient ship with sails appears on the crest of a wave and disappears in the swell forever. We briefly hear sailors shouting in the distance over the moving curtain sounds of rain,
> Tie him to the mast!
> Tie him to the mast!

The Odysseus/Ulysseus Myth disappears into THE DEEP before we have time to grasp it... but the Unconscious holds it. He is one of the few Mythic Heroes to successfully journey to the Underworld and back. {Remember this day!}

The dark watery turbulence begins to flatten out as dawn breaks into peaceful silence.

Elegant words in light appear:

I Shall Tell The Land Of The One Who Learned All Things.

Fade to next words:

Of The One Who Experienced Everything.

Fade to next words:

I Shall Teach The Whole.

Fade to next:

He Searched Lands Everywhere.

Fade to next:

He Found Out What Was Secret And Uncovered What Was Hidden.

Fade to next:

He Brought Back Tales Of Times Before The Flood.

Gilgamesh 2600 BC

The bright dawn appears over the ocean, illuminating land in the distance. The unknown observer, whose nose is just above the dark waters of the Collective Unconscious, slowly looks up into the sky as if to search space itself. Blue turns to black as we travel the Other DEEP.

Stars appear, moving past us on all sides. We find ourselves moving along behind a rare Ataxite meteorite, all sixty tons of it.

Screen words appear:

20,000 BC

Out of the darkness we see the small blue ball of Earth draw nearer and nearer. The meteorite comes out from THE DEEP and enters the Earth's atmosphere on fire!

It explodes just before impact. Molten pieces of nickel-iron splatter everywhere!

Screen words read:

SIBERIAN-MONGOLIAN BORDER

We come down gently from the aerial view to see the landscape smoldering from the human eye level above ground. We see a person on either side of us on foot. We hear them huffing and puffing. They are wearing Scythian type clothing. It is thick and long, comfortable attire, to brace against the cold.

One man reaches down and pries a warm elongated chunk out of the Earth. It is about one foot long and twenty five pounds. Gingerly, he wraps it in a cloth and steals off with it in hand.

Black stallions are galloping and streaking across the mountain. Wild horses and baby colts frolic. The air is fresh and alive. It is a good day for all.

INT. WORK SHOP - 20,000 BC

We see all kinds of statues and statuettes around the rather large shop. Most of them are of the sacred God type from around the ancient pre-deluge world. Some are prayerful practitioner statues. They are surprisingly more realistic, powerful and graceful, just as the Greek and Roman styles are known to be. Even the Buddhist style statues, standing and cross-legged, are supremely proportional.

The steles are much more like Ancient Sumerian than Egyptian but also with more realistic details. There is no crude cuneiform here, but a graceful symbology and lettering. Many of the statues and steles have small Z-shaped swastikas formed on them representing the creative force of the Universe. None of them have the S-shaped swastika of destruction and demise.

The same man who rescued the smoldering chunk is in a chair chiseling some last delicate details on the ten inch Ataxite meteorite known today as Iron Man. The rare high nickle content makes it much easier to tool and craft.

He leans backward, almost satisfied with his work. He thoughtfully chants over his prayer beads in hand.

We have a full view of the statue. His right hand is palm out in blessing and his left hand holds a fruit of Immortality. Moving closer and closer to the center of the cross-legged Iron Man figure, we can now clearly see the four directional creation swastika projecting out from his heart.

We move close enough that everything turns to DEEP black.

Now, the Hubble shot of the Eye Of God nebula in space comes into view.

Words appear below its mesmerizing glow:

SHA NAQBA IMURRU

HE WHO SAW THE DEEP

Shadows of shamanic dancers arc over the Eye Of God. Shadowy spirit warriors dance and fight and die and resurrect and embrace, transforming into each other as they dance again and again in the round of Earth's history. They are indeed all of us, dancing through our painstaking evolution.

AIKEN ELEMENTARY SCHOOL - SOUTH CAROLINA - SEPTEMBER 1961

We see kids running around a small town school yard. Girls are playing hopscotch. Some are jump roping, others are playing string games... Boys are running around diving after basketballs.

We see awkward Simon, moving ungainly through the kids. No one really talks to him. Pan over to a larger set boy - tall, Germanic looking, big boned. Eleven years of age. Many around him are ten.

> DANNY
> Robert, you're on our team!

> ROBERT
> They need me over there.

> DANNY
> Ahh, come on, Robert! They have Bill and John. Be on our side!

> ROBERT
> {Grimacing} Yeah, I guess.

> SIMON
> What about me?

Danny gives Simon the once over and turns his back to him. He nonchalantly starts whistling as he strides mid court when the boy lurches near him, trying to grab the rubber ball.

Danny stiffs him and dances the ball around Simon's body easily. The boy thrusts out his arms and smiles at Danny while Danny spins the ball on one finger.

> SIMON (CONT'D)
> Ball, I want the ball! Come on! Give me the ball!

> DANNY
> You want the ball, huh?

Simon smiles at him, beaming and arms open wide. Something about him is a little off. Danny smiles back at Simon.

> DANNY (CONT'D)
> Beg! Get down on your knees and beg!

> SIMON
> Ball! Gi... give me the ball... ball, please.

> ROBERT
> What are you doing, Danny?

> DANNY
> The retard wants the ball. I just think he needs to do a little begging.

                    ROBERT
          Ahh, come on, Danny! Give him the
          stupid ball.

Simon watches, his eyes still bright and lively.

                    DANNY
          Yeah, you want the ball?

Simon starts nodding his head furiously. Danny laughs and
then lightning quick, hurls the ball hard at Simon's stomach.
Simon collapses on the concrete, writhing in agony.

                    MIKE
          Wha'd you do that for?

                    DANNY
          He bugs me, Mike.

Mike runs and retrieves the ball. A small group of kids
surround Simon. Simon is taking in shaky breaths and tears
are running down his cheeks. Danny approaches them.

                    DANNY (CONT'D)
          Mike! Give it here!

Mike tightens his lip as he looks into Simon's eyes. Simon is
trembling and too scared to get up. Robert walks over to him
and offers him his hand.

                    ROBERT
          Here, Simon. Take my hand.

Simon is up. Danny, with a scowl, pokes the rubber ball from
under Mike's arm and then trips and shoves him into Simon.
Now they are both down. Some of the kids start laughing.

                    DANNY
          Hey, we got two retards here! They
          gonna get married or what?

As the kids chortle, Danny swings his leg and gives Mike a
vicious kick in the stomach while he is still down.

                    DANNY (CONT'D)
          You two deserve each other.

                    ROBERT
          Hey, cut it out!

                    DANNY
          What are you gonna do? You gonna
          stop me?

Robert stares back at Danny but looks uncertain. Mike gets up and lunges at Danny but Danny punches him right in the nose. Blood spurts out on Mike's shirt as he falls down again.

          DANNY (CONT'D)
    Oh, my, oh, my! What have we done?
    Looks like you got yourself a
    bloody nose. Think twice before you
    take me on!

Robert stares long and hard at Danny. He then turns his back on him and helps Mike up on his feet.

          ROBERT
    Stand by me and he won't hurt you!

          MIKE
    Buds forever?

          ROBERT
    Buds forever!

Danny clenches his fists several times but hesitates to cross that invisible line with Robert. Many another boy has tasted his fury before graduation, but something was different when it came to Robert... Something familiar was in those eyes.

DIRT ROAD - SOUTH CAROLINA - LATER THAT AFTERNOON

We see Robert's shoes pushing through a dusty road. He's trudging by some trees, DEEP in thought.

          DANNY
    Hey, Robert! Wait up!

Robert turns around and sees Danny running up to him.

          DANNY (CONT'D)
    Hey... I guess I kinda got carried
    away.

Danny searches Robert's face as Robert looks at him impassively.

          DANNY (CONT'D)
    I don't know what it is, but Simon
    gives me the creeps. He just bugs
    me... Shoot, he's too stupid!

A blue '55 Ford convertible drives up, spewing swirls of dirt and dust around the boys. A man in his thirties pokes his head out and spits some tobacco in their direction.

                        MR. CROWLEY
            Dammit, Danny! Where the hell you
            been? I told ya I was pickin' you
            up! How goddamn stupid can you be?
            Git in here now!

                        DANNY
            Sorry, Sir... sorry.

Danny scrambles around the car.

                        MR.CROWLEY
            Yeah, yeah. {Sizes Robert up} What
            kind of company you been keepin'?

                        ROBERT
            Afternoon, sir.

                        MR.CROWLEY
            You got a name?

                        ROBERT
            Robert. Sir.

Crowley narrows his eyes and stares right through Robert. With a grunt, father and son fly out of there like good ol' boys do in THE DEEP South, sending plumes of dirt and dust into Robert's face.

EXT. SHERWOOD FOREST

{Interactive note: While reading this scene, use your device to google "pink floyd grantchester meadows youtube." Play the studio version from 3:45 to 6:50.}

At the entrance to Sherwood Forest is a simple wooden welcome sign. There are no cars parked in the small dirt parking lot, if you can call it a parking lot.

Robert walks across a sand patch to the trees and breathes out DEEPLY. Breathing in the sweet air, he starts making his way through the trees, eventually picking his way over some boulders.

Grantchester Meadows: "All around me golden sunflakes settle on the ground, basking in the sunshine of a by gone afternoon."

Robert hears a croak and scrambles around the marsh before finally capturing a baby bullfrog. Delighted, he slowly opens his fist.

8.

                    ROBERT (CONT'D)
              Hey, look at you! How ya doin?

He plays with the frog and even stuffs it into his pocket before deciding to just let it go. He continues to hike through the forest, and climbs up a tree to survey part of the forest.

Grantchester Meadows: "And a river of green is sliding unseen beneath the trees, laughing as it passes through the endless summer making for the sea."

Next to him, he spies a centipede and picks it up and puts it in his hand. Lost in thought on the limb, he starts counting the legs.

The guitars stop playing in Grantchester Meadows and the fly is predominant. The song stops suddenly before the swat...

EXT. SILVER SAUCER

A dark shape passes over his palm. Robert looks up and finds himself staring at a saucer shaped silver disc whirring above him in the pre-dusk sky. Cringing down, he slides down the trunk of the tree and holds himself still. The saucer pulls away and then pans over to him.

                    ROBERT (CONT'D)
              Oh, no.

Robert darts among the bushes and heads DEEPER into the woods. The saucer is still pursuing him.

EXT. RED BARN CONVERTED TO STOREHOUSE

Robert crashes through the bushes and suddenly comes across a large red barn. The saucer is panning back and forth among the trees near the river. Robert runs headlong toward the barn. A tractor beam is now searching to capture him. He just escapes it under the protection of the tiny door awning.

INT. RED BARN

Rushing in and looking around the large space, Robert finds a door to a little office room. He opens it and lurches in only to find himself staring into the DEEP open eyes of a six foot Being standing in the middle of the room! He would pass as a normal human under normal circumstances... except for those eyes! Those large piercing eyes! No hiding in here!

Robert backs up to leave but the door slams shut by the slightly glowing hand of another being who has been behind the door. Robert slowly realizes that he has them right where they want him, as Captain Kirk once wryly said, a few years after this experience! This was all a setup to get Robert into the barn! They knew he would bolt and hide so a couple of them were already in wait for him here!

The Being sees Robert is in fear and speaks in tones of soft sound as it touches Robert's head and heart. Robert listens and relaxes with understanding as the Being looks DEEP inside him, asking questions as if Robert was their family member.

INT. BEDROOM - NEXT MORNING

Sun splashes over Robert as he yawns and looks around his bedroom slightly puzzled. He shakes his head.

          ROBERT
What a crazy dream! I think? I don't remember walking home last night. It must have been a dream!

The alarm clock sounds. Robert shuts it off and dresses for school.

INT. CLASSROOM

The chalk on the black board behind the teacher reads:

6th Grade   Today is Friday, September 22, 1961

More chalk dashes: This year John F. Kennedy is the 35th President of the United States of America. Current History: July 25th Kennedy urged Americans to build fallout shelters as one important step in Civil Defense.

          MRS. DOBBS
Open your math books to page 35. We will review some of last years work before we move on. We will start off with multiplication. Sarah, start with number 1, and we will continue down the row.

          SARAH
4 times 6 = 24

          MRS. DOBBS
Correct. Jason?

JASON
3 times 7 = 21

MRS. DOBBS
Very good. Simon?

Simon stands up, smiling but a little disconcerted. He has a cut over his eye and a slight bruise. Danny has been silently distracting him on purpose.

MRS. DOBBS (CONT'D)
Do you know where we are, Simon?

DANNY
He thinks he's in a zoo!

Scattered laughter. Mrs. Dobbs ignores Danny.

MRS. DOBBS
Have you been paying attention?

SIMON
Yess... yes, Ma... Ma'am.

MRS. DOBBS
Then where are we?

Robert is scanning Mrs. Dobbs' face and sees a darkening around her.

SIMON
Num... num... num...

DANNY
Num... num... num...

Suppressed giggling dances out around the whole class.

SIMON
Ber... fo... four

MRS. DOBBS
Yes, well, what is it?

DANNY
Four!!!

Danny half stands and swings a make believe golf club. Simon looks over at Danny's smirking face and freezes. Bursts of laughter erupt around him.

MRS. DOBBS
The answer, Simon?!

Robert puts up his hand.

                    MRS. DOBBS (CONT'D)
          Robert?

                    ROBERT
          Why do you let Danny bully Simon?
          He already beat him up yesterday.
          Why don't you stop him?

Mrs. Dobbs gives him a stern look that could kill flies innocently passing by her head of tightly bound hair.

                    MRS. DOBBS
          Are you questioning me?

Robert stares at her with an intense yet astonished look in his face.

                    MRS. DOBBS (CONT'D)
          Are you questioning me?

Danny rolls his head sidewards to casually look at Robert.

                    DANNY
          What's your problem? You don't like
          us picking on retard here?

Decision time here. Robert sees red but quickly regains composure.

                    ROBERT
          What you're doing is wrong. What
          all of you are doing is wrong!

There is a silence in the room as Mrs. Dobbs looks at Robert and then at the floor. The bell rings.

EXT. SWING - SATURDAY AFTERNOON - NEXT DAY - SEPT. 23RD

Robert is outside in his backyard. He watches as his neighbors put the finishing touches to a tall, definitely not standard, swing set they fashioned out of wood pillars.

INT. BEDROOM - EVENING

Robert is fooling around in his room and then becomes drawn to the window to look outside. He stares at the swing set.

EXT. BACKYARD SWING - SUNDAY MORNING

The neighbors have left for church. Robert's mom is ill so he has a rare stay at home. No one is watching when Robert slips out and approaches the forbidden swing set. He cautiously sits down on the swing. Looking over his shoulder, he is at first tentative and then loosens up and begins to swirl around in the swing.

POV ROBERT LOOKING OUTWARD FROM THE SWING

The world careens in jumbled greens and blues from the sky and sunshine. Abruptly, Robert breaks out and starts pumping his legs to swing higher and higher and even higher.

MRS. DOBBS - KITCHEN - SAME DAY - SEPT. 24TH

Mrs. Dobbs is placing bread in the toaster. Her friend is seated at the table, eyeing her and sipping the ritual Sunday cup of coffee.

> MURIEL
> What's got into you, Nancy? You seem kinda jittery.

> MRS. DOBBS
> This boy... {Shakes her head} from the mouth of babes... {Sits down heavily} I messed up, Muriel. I really messed up.

POV ROBERT LOOKING OUTWARD FROM THE SWING

Robert is really soaring now. The air is rushing past and blowing his hair up and he just breathes it all in, raptured in a rhythmic dance. The swing glides higher and higher.

COLLECTIVE SOUL plays Shine: "Lay me on the ground, fly me in the sky, show me where to look, tell me what will I find? Oh, Heaven let your light shine down!"

SLOW MOTION SWING

Suddenly, the rope becomes slack. He has swung too high and now everything is collapsing. Slowly, Robert is propelled backward and down, incredibly just missing the top bar. Down he goes until he becomes "impaled" upon a huge scuff log laying half imbedded in the ground below the swing. He is startled, his eyes wide in amazement. Flat out on the ground, he stares at the sky. He can't move at all.

CLOSE UP ROBERT

Robert tries to breathe in but can only breathe out. He is astonished and tries to gain his breath but instead feels his world stretching out beneath him. His diaphragm is in shock and is no longer working. He realizes he's dying. He takes in one long last look at life from his frozen spot.

LOOKING UP THROUGH TREES

A wave ripples out in the air as his vision expands. A symphony of trees and birds, butterflies and sunshine abounds. The trees are greener and the sky is bluer. The trees and sky are singing with vibrancy. Everything is alive with joy. Robert hears a thunderous voice in the sky asking, "Huuu are youuu?" With this, his mind switches focus.

EXT. HISTORICAL IMPRINT - 1200 AD

Long term memories are stored out in nature. Robert sees a Native American and then another tracking through the forest. They are smelling the rich old peat of the earth. They can even distinguish the different scents of the tree bark. They are happy, alert and engaged with life.

EXT. HISTORICAL IMPRINT - 1625 AD

The scene shifts and Robert sees a few Indians surrounding a campfire. They are laughing and enjoying a meal together. A frontiersman signals his trapper friends and they storm the campfire. The Indians are killed and the hungry men eat ravenously at the food that is roasting.

EXT. HISTORICAL IMPRINT - FEBRUARY 11, 1865

The Battle of Aiken, South Carolina. A soldier in gray slinks forward in the grass. Behind him are other buddies. Before them Cavalry soldiers cautiously approach with their rifles held firmly in their hands... Suddenly, a Confederate soldier signals his comrades and with a whoop, they fire in unison and take down three Union soldiers.

Other Union soldiers press behind the trees and start firing. One Confederate soldier rushes in and bayonets a Union soldier. The Union soldier screams in agony and his cry infuriates his fellow soldiers. It is a brutal scene. But they are all dead and long gone... and now, Robert is dead too. He is released from pain, released from the past and now, released from the bonds of the Earth.

CURRENT DAY - ROBERT - 1961

Robert is floating in the sky. He is passing through the different layers of the atmosphere like a dandelion seed-puff floating upward in the gentle breeze. He is filled with a DEEP love beyond any human love he has ever felt. He is totally elated and trusting.

The long note of a didgeridoo is heard. The whole world can be seen and everyone is wailing with mud on their faces. Robert feels the world's pain. Then he hears a thunderous voice in the sky asking, "Whaaat do you waaant?"

CLOSE UP - ROBERT ON GROUND

A sudden gush of air floods into Robert's lungs and his Soul becomes flattened and still inside his body. He starts to move his hands.

          ROBERT
I'm alive! I can't believe!
I am alive!!

A soft refrain from BIFF ROSE's Children Of Light plays: "Are you a child of Light? Are we children of Light? Just ask and receive, yourself, you must ask and receive. The children of Light will be permitted to look through each other's eyes."

FAMILY DINNER TABLE

Family is seated at the table: Mom and Dad, three brothers and a sister. Everyone is eating and mom is giving the eldest child Robert, a conspiratorial smile.

          MOM
Guess who called me up today...
you'll never guess. {The family
looks around at each other}

          DAD
Does it have to do with school?

          MOM
I'm not telling.

          BROTHER
Well, whatever it is, I didn't do it.

She is too beside herself to not say anything more.

                    MOM
          Mrs. Dobbs called...

                    BROTHER
          Oh wow. You're in it now, Robert.

                    MOM
          {Beaming} She said you spoke up for
          someone in class. Do you remember?
          What happened?

                    ROBERT
          I don't know.

Mom gives Robert a searching look.

                    ROBERT (CONT'D)
          Some kid was picking on another
                    kid...

                    BROTHER
          {Interrupting} It was Danny, wasn't
          it? What a bully!

                    ROBERT
          I just said... that... that it
          ought to stop.

Mom is on a roll now, and cannot stop herself.

                    MOM
          Well, it certainly impressed Mrs.
          Dobbs! You know what she said?...
          She said that with your sense of
          honesty and fairness, she sees you
          becoming the President of the
          United States some day! Just like
          Abraham Lincoln!

                    DAD
          What?? That was nice of her!

                    BROTHER
          Yea, well, wait till they find out
          about the swing!

                    ROBERT
          Donald!!!

ROBERT'S BEDROOM - EARLY NEXT SATURDAY MORNING

Robert is staring out the window looking at the swing set. The swing is lightly tilting in the breeze. The trees are gently swaying, their leaves fluttering through filtered streams of light. It begins to rain. The sky turns dark. The rain turns into a downpour. Robert just keeps staring out the window lost in thought. The sound of the water fills his Soul. Robert gets up and slips under the covers of his bed again. He falls asleep.

ROBERT'S DREAMSCAPE

Robert is standing on the beach. The mighty towers of Atlantis are behind him. He walks into the ocean and shallow dives. He swims out a couple hundred yards before diving straight under. He swims DEEPER and DEEPER when the continental plates slip by the shoreline, one under the other.

The mighty towers of Atlantis rock and sway. The land drops several feet and a tsunami wave rolls in and surges at least a third of the way up the tallest sky scrapers.

Robert, DEEP down on the other side of this is thrashed for a bit but continues to swim down to the ocean floor, finding that he can now breathe under water.

As he glides the bottom, he finds a ring and puts it on a finger. He finds another and another until he has four rings on his left hand and three rings on his right. He swims up to the sunlight with ease.

Robert wakes up on his back now moving his arms in the air as if still swimming. He realizes where he is, stops abruptly, then moves his hands toward his face to get a closer look at his fingers.

                      ROBERT
Doggone it! I swear I brought these seven rings back with me!

And with a determined look on his face...

                      ROBERT (CONT'D)
I k<u>now </u>I did!

MONTAGE: ELEMENTARY - JUNIOR HIGH - HIGH SCHOOL

Robert is walking through the Elementary School hall. Various students peer at him. There is fear, wonder and curiosity in their eyes as he passes them.

Robert looks at them and sees mud superimposed on their faces. Some have more mud than others. The mud represents layers of personality and protection caked over original innocence and authenticity. Popularity rules the day.

He passes by Mrs. Dobbs correcting papers at her desk. She looks over at him. There is mud on her face, but tears have washed some of the debris away.

Robert is walking through the Junior High School hallway. We start to hear the first strains of the STONES "Gimme Shelter" play as a clique of girls meet by some lockers. A plump girl approaches and one girl, a cheer leader, makes some snide remark and starts laughing. The others start laughing as well... ROLLING STONES: "Oh, a storm is threatening my very life today, if I don't get some shelter, oh yeah, I'm gonna fade away."

Robert is in a High School history class. The music becomes louder as we see the class discussing national and world events. Images of a naked ten year old Vietnamese girl crying and screaming from the napalm streaming off her flesh is juxtaposed with muddied faces, burning cities, police pulling and pushing in a maze of black and white demonstrators. High school kids are bullying and tearing each other down...

We hear Robert's heart beat get louder and louder as the dizzying array of images {including the Kennedy assassination} streak faster into a claustrophobic cluster. These three time periods are all meant to build upon each other to culminate into an overwhelming sense of hell.

ROLLING STONES Gimme Shelter is embedded: "It's just a shot away! It's just a shot away... It's just a kiss away."

In the very last scene of this montage, Robert is pulling a young boy off another student. Macabre faces caked with mud are laughing then crying then hurling insults.

ROBERT'S BEDROOM - DAYLIGHT - 1967

The last lyrics of Gimme Shelter fade away as we see Robert writing on a pad of paper. His eyes are wet and he looks morose. Carefully, he places the letter in the second drawer of the desk. He approaches his window and looks out at the swing. He smiles and inhales. Gathering his jacket, he steps out into the bright sunshine.

THE WATER TOWER - AFTERNOON

The wind is whipping at his jacket as Robert heads out to a field and begins walking towards a large water tower.

KING CRIMSON's Epitaph begins: "The wall on which the prophets wrote is cracking at the seams."

Springing lightly to the first rung, Robert easily climbs to the very top of the 132 foot tower. It's not his first time.

K. C. Epitaph: "Between the iron gates of Fate, the seeds of time were sown, and watered by the deeds of those who Know and who are known."

Robert takes a moment to survey the blue sky and the world laid out in front of him. The homes look peaceful and far away, a little girl is riding a powder pink bike.

K. C. Epitaph: "The Fate of all Mankind I see, is in the hands of fools."

Robert smiles ever so briefly as he watches the little girl.

>   ROBERT
> One person alone cannot save the
> world. It's too big and there's too
> much mud. They don't even realize
> they lost who they are.

...And he jumps.

POV ON WATER TOWER - ROBERT LOOKING DOWN

We see a perpendicular view of the little girl bike riding abruptly vertical. We hear Robert's breath and a strange whirring sound as we see the world through his eyes plummeting. At an arc, we see a silver oval shaped disc cut in rapidly. The sky and ground and trees and the town itself shimmer back upon themselves from the oval surface.

POV ROBERT IN AIR - RIPPLING EFFECT

We see Robert's body moving slightly upward through a ripple of light. As he drifts in slow motion he sees his potential future in front of him. A blonde flaxen haired young woman with eyes on fire is coming toward him from out of the ocean.

She grabs his right hand with her left hand and they fly out toward the sun together.

People with mud on their faces are down below on the shore reaching out to the couple who left them. They are wailing.

Our couple's legs come into view. Ankle chains are seen shaking, as if ready to fall off the ankles.

A motorcycle is hit by a white Toyota and the bike's extended exhaust pipes break off and go flying. "None of this makes sense," is reflected on Robert's face.

POV UFO INTERIOR - DRENCHED IN WHITENESS

Vision is clear now. Everything is white around Robert. We see again into the eyes of an adult alien being - the same alien being that first met with Robert as a child. We see by the eyes of the being, the tone and the sound emanating from this being, that it is really concerned and upset with him. It shakes its head at him and gestures at the outside world.

Robert listens and then responds in kind, using similar sound emanations. An understanding is finally reached.

POV ROBERT IN AIR - RIPPLING EFFECT

Robert's body is moving downward through another ripple of light in slow motion.

EXT. BASE OF WATER TOWER

Robert's back hits the ground with a thud. He stares transfixed as a thin flare of light disappears toward the East. He feels his head and his legs for damage, then spots the powder pink bike. The little girl is playing on the lawn with a puppy and another little girl. She is shrieking and laughing as the puppy trips her and then pounces on her, licking her face. Robert thoughtfully exhales, slowly rises and walks away from the tower.

HIGH SCHOOL MYTHOLOGY CLASS - 1968

The blackboard has "Class of '68" across the top. Below there is: Those Who Sought Immortality- Gilgamesh- Ponce de Leon- Alexander The Great- Qin Shi Huang, 1st Emperor of China.

The teacher is reading then reacting to Robert's summary of The Adventures Of Ulysses to the class.

> TEACHER
> What kind of cockamamy theory is this? {Class laughs} Ulysses represents every man's potential? {Class laughs louder} As does Superman? {Sighs} Well, at least I will give you a "D" for creativity.

                    DANNY
          Teach'! You should give him an "A"
          for imagination! {Class howls}

Robert shakes his head like some things just don't change.

EXT. GRADUATION - FOOTBALL FIELD

Parents are in the old wooden bleachers. We see rows upon rows of lawn chairs on the field with graduates seated and listening to a speaker at the podium.

                 VALEDICTORIAN
          And why? Because we are the class
          of '68! The important things we've
          learned, we can do now. We've come
          a long way from where we were as
          freshmen. So now here we stand,
          proud and ready to make our mark on
          the world. What shall it be? Think
          long and hard on it, for we can do
          anything. We are the class of 1968!
          Graduates, flip those tassels to
          the right! Come on, world!!!

With a whoop, the graduates stand up and throw their graduation caps into the air.

EXT. SLOW MOTION SHOT

We see the sun lighting up the tassels as the square caps rise and fall against the clear blue sky.

EXT. MOTORCYCLE RACE - SUMMER - 1972

                    ROBERT
          Look ma, no hands!

Robert is shouting back to a motorcyclist over the roar of his 305 Yamaha. His hands are in the air, celebrating.

Clint is trailing behind him on his own 650 Yamaha on the roller-coaster winding country road.

                    CLINT
          Show-off!!

                    ROBERT
          Hey! You lost!... OH!

Robert is going too fast around a curve and is forced into the thick woods because his kick stand mount struck the ground. He was leaning so low! We see branches brush his arms. His eyes are wide open and his mouth is tight. It is just a wall of trees. It is an impossible task yet, he comes out safely through the unplanned shortcut to the road again.

                CLINT
Man, you're nuts!

                ROBERT
{Laughing} You had your chance!

                CLINT
Yeah, but you're crazy! How'd you do that?

                ROBERT
305 Yamaha bored out to a 355!

                CLINT
No wonder! But, no! I mean, how did you get through the woods in one piece? There is no clearance!

                ROBERT
Providence!

                CLINT
Providence, my ass! But you're still crazy! Certifiably crazy!

Robert laughs heartily. Clint shakes his head. Robert bursts ahead and Clint catches up.

                CLINT (CONT'D)
Doing wheelies in third gear too? You got to be kidding! Got any kids?

                ROBERT
Come on, what do you think?

                CLINT
You got a woman?

                ROBERT
Nope. Not lookin' neither!

                CLINT
Listen, you got to come over and meet my old lady. You like catfish, doncha?

                    ROBERT
          Oh, yeah.

                    CLINT
          Sherrie cooks up a mean catfish
          dinner. Hey, why not come over
          tonight? We can catch up on old
          times.

                    ROBERT
          Sounds good to me... long as that's
          all you're cookin' up.

                    CLINT
          You know me.

                    ROBERT
          Yeah, that's what's got me worried.

                    CLINT
          You, worried? I don't think so.
          {Winks at him and then scribbles
          down an address} Is seven okay with
          you?

                    ROBERT
          Sure.

                    CLINT
          See you then.

ROBERT'S BEDROOM

Robert is just buttoning up a leather jacket as he stands before a mirror. From the corner of his eye he spots a three inch shaft of light that curls in on itself and shifts through the ceiling. He stares at the exit location for a second, hesitates at the sign, and then walks out the door.

CLINT'S HOUSE

Sherrie is shaking herbs over frying catfish as her friend, Kathy, searches for plates. Excitement rules the evening.

                    CLINT
          So, I figure it's been... what...
          six years since...

                    SHERRIE
          {Injects} Has Mark changed much?

                        KATHY
            No, he's still the same. He
            still...

They hear knocking on the door. Clint moves to the front door
and opens it.

                        CLINT
            Hey, buddy.

                        ROBERT
            Hey.

                        CLINT
            Come in. Hey everybody! This here
            is Robert! Robert, meet Sherrie,
            the love of my life!

A very pregnant Sherrie peeps out from the kitchen and gives
Robert a wide smile as she wipes her hands on her apron.

                        SHERRIE
            So you're the notorious Robert
            Penhaligon. I got flour all over
            me, if you'll excuse the mess.

                        ROBERT
            {Shaking hands} I so appreciate
            anybody making a mess to cook
            catfish! It smells great!

                        SHERRIE
            Why, thank-you! You're so sweet!
            And this here is my friend, Kathy.

Kathy looks up from pouring sweet tea and smiles at Robert.
Robert instinctively rolls his eyes realizing he has been set
up by Clint. Set up by the curl of light too!

                        KATHY
            Nice to meet you.

                        ROBERT
            Hi...

Their eyes meet. Everything around them fades away. She sees
a ball of blue light come out from his forehead and crash
into hers. She is visibly taken back. Robert thinks perhaps
she doesn't like him and realizes he is staring and turns to
Sherrie.

                        ROBERT (CONT'D)
            Did you say deviled eggs, Sherrie?

SHERRIE
Only in your imagination! But Clint told me they were your favorite!

ROBERT
{Feigning disappointment} Oh, man!

SHERRIE
Everything is done, {Walks out with a tray} including the deviled eggs!

ROBERT
{Delighted} Oh, wow! I am in love! {Blows her a kiss} Thank you!

SHERRIE
{Smiles} let's dig in, shall we? Here, everybody grab a plate and the salad is over there. Kathy makes the best salad ever!

CLINT
Just leave me some avocados, that's all I ask!

KATHY
Here, Robert, you can start first.

ROBERT
No problem! {Sneaks a deviled egg and pops it in his mouth}

SHERRIE
Carpe Diem, honey!

Robert looks at Kathy, half-smiles and heads for the catfish. The others follow suit, chattering as they pile on the food.

CLINT
So did you ride your bike over here?

ROBERT
Well, I didn't come by cab!

KATHY
Wow, you like to ride motorcycles, huh?

Robert glances over at her, noticing the light wisp of color highlighting her long, flowing hair. It seems familiar somehow.

ROBERT
Yeah, it's all I got... and need.

SHERRIE
What kind of bike you ride?

ROBERT
305... Yamaha.

SHERRIE
How fun. I always thought it would be cool to own a bike.

CLINT
Keep dreamin' honey 'cause you're not going anywhere with that big belly.

People are sitting down at the table.

ROBERT
You ever ride a motorcycle, Kathy?

KATHY
Nope. Not even sat behind someone driving one.

This bit of information unnerves Robert. He hesitates as Clint rolls his eyes at Robert and silently mouths "Take her!" Robert looks startled, catches Sherrie's smiling eyes, looks down quickly and pokes at the catfish. He is thinking they are in it together, great! Is Kathy too? He struggles to keep his cool.

ROBERT
This looks really good.

CLINT
Hey God! Bless this food and bless us with your presence inside and outside and all around us Amen!

Everyone choruses "Amen!" They all begin to slice and pick at their plates with agreeable tones.

Kathy gives Robert a tentative smile.

KATHY
Why do you have a motorcycle? Aren't they dangerous?

ROBERT
No more dangerous than me.

Robert digs into the catfish, savoring the flavor of both the food and his wry humor. Sherry tries quickly to divert perceived impending disaster.

                    SHERRIE
          Soooo, Clint. So who's sayin' I've
          got a BIG BELLY?

                    CLINT
          Oh Lord...

                    ROBERT
          Soo what do you do for work, Kathy?

                    KATHY
          Well, it's not like I get paid.

                    ROBERT
          Yeah?

                    SHERRIE
          Oh, come on, Kathy. What's money
          got to do with it? She goes to the
          Humane Society in the morning,
          walks homeless dogs and plays with
          homeless cats. Picks up their dog
          and cat shit. {Squints at Kathy}
          How many cats you got now, Kath?

                    ROBERT
          You work at the Humane Society? So
          how long have you been in Aiken? I
          haven't seen you around here
          before.

                    KATHY
          Just a couple of months. I'm just
          now finding my way around.

                    ROBERT
          Where did you come in from?

                    KATHY
          Iowa. Same as Sherrie and Clint.

                    ROBERT
          Did you move down here by yourself?

Kathy and Sherrie exchange uneasy glances which is not lost on Robert.

                    ROBERT (CONT'D)
          I hope I'm not stepping on
          anybody's toes, here.

Kathy and Sherrie both start talking at the same time and then stop. Kathy takes the lead.

                      KATHY
          I came out here to make this place
          my home.

                    SHERRIE
          Robert, would you care for another
          glass of sweet tea?

The group finish eating and move to the living room.

                    CLINT
          Yeah, well, those demonstrations
          can get pretty hairy. Remember
          Charles? Got his head beat in on
          the Berkeley campus... never been
          the same since.

                    SHERRIE
          But Charlie is so confrontational!

                    CLINT
          Don't you get it? Police are pigs.
          They tear gassed them! They clubbed
          them, they killed them! Kent State,
          Watts, Peoples Park... and don't
          you even think about going on any
          march around here, Sherrie! You're
          pregnant. Anything could happen.
          You're not going and that's final!

Clint offers Robert a burning joint. Robert waves it off as he speaks.

                    ROBERT
          Food is a pleasant drug. Life
          itself is a drug. Culture is a drug
          programmed into us.

Clint tries to pass on the marijuana, but Sherrie is pregnant and Kathy is not interested.

                    SHERRIE
          Riots and war are real. Can you
          believe we are still in Vietnam?

                    KATHY
          I know! I wish more people would
          side with peace.

CLINT
I think they have. It is just the Establishment, the Man, slowing us down.

ROBERT
Power and greed. Absolute power corrupts absolutely.

KATHY
Why are people so selfish? Can't we just all get along?

CLINT
We need a young Democrat elected President.

ROBERT
Both parties are just as corrupt in their own polarized ways. We need a new party of visionaries and no more violent revolutionaries.

CLINT
Why don't you run for President when you turn 35?

ROBERT
Unfortunately, I'm not interested in man's law, stock markets, or politics... And remember Robert Kennedy was assassinated in '68, less than three months after announcing he was going to run!

KATHY
What *are* you interested in?

ROBERT
Truth. The ultimately highest, naked truth! Society is primmed, primed and programmed for power and wealth in the name of self interest. I seek the Ultimate Nature of man. Truth, Wisdom, clarity, vision... Eternity!

An ice cube cracks in Robert's sweet tea. A drop splatters on the middle of his forehead.

CLINT
I will show you Eternity! This hell on Earth! That's Eternity! Wars, poverty, disease.

CLINT (CONT'D)
The Establishment has its hidden agendas and special interest groups.

SHERRIE
Whoa, baby, whoa! You'll end up like Charlie and that's no good!

KATHY
We need love on Earth, not fear and mistrust.

ROBERT
I am done with politicians. I am done with Institutions. I am done with Western religions. They have carried me to the end of the road and there is nothing substantial inside. I hunger for more. Ultimate reality. Ultimate truth. We must follow ourselves and no one else. No one else can get us there!

Another ice cube cracks this time in Kathy's sweet tea. A drop splatters on the middle of her forehead.

KATHY
I tasted some of that.

ROBERT
Some of what?

KATHY
My Self, my reality.

ROBERT
How did you do that?

KATHY
I was in a Kundalini ashram for {Flashback is seen while she talks} the last year and learned how to trigger energy in my body that seemed to help me explore myself.

ROBERT
There you go! That is something I want to look into, the Kundalini! Meditation is one thing. Kundalini must be a very active trigger with the power of breath!... Intense oxygen...

Kathy nods her head while Sherrie loses interest and interrupts.

>   SHERRIE
>   Hey, I'm dyin' to go for a swim!
>   It's just too hot right now.

>   CLINT
>   Hey, baby, nobody's holding you
>   back.

EXT. POOL - NIGHT LIGHTING

The four are in the pool. Clint is splashing Sherrie as she shrieks and demands that he stops.

>   SHERRIE
>   You're ruining my hair!!! Stop it!
>   Stop it or I'll...

>   CLINT
>   Or you'll what? Just what are you
>   {Splashes her} going to {Splashes
>   her} do {Splash} to me?

>   SHERRIE
>   {Shrieks} Clint, dammit! I just got
>   my hair done! Clint!!!

Robert blind-sides Clint with a couple of splashes of his own. Clint counters and splashes back. Kathy gets into the fray, splashing both Clint and Robert.

Sherrie scrambles out of the pool desperately dabbing at her hair, but Clint chases her back inside the house, mercilessly teasing her.

Robert is now splashing Kathy and she is splashing back. They both dash out of the pool, laughing and chasing each other.

An older couple looking on from a third story balcony start laughing gently and talking in whispers about their own once youthful play.

Kathy dives from the cool deck into the shallow end as Robert dives from across the pool.

They both almost collide underwater and she instinctively grabs his right hand with her left. They start swimming underwater towards the round pool light below the diving board area.

Robert flashes on the water tower vision of the flaxen haired girl reaching for his hand and flying toward the sun. That is why she looks so familiar! He keeps this to himself.

INT. LIVING ROOM

Clint is picking at the left over food. Kathy towels her hair as Sherry watches.

> KATHY
> Why did you two just disappear?

> CLINT
> It was Sherrie's idea.

> SHERRIE
> You two looked like you needed to... you know... spend some time together.

> CLINT
> Well, do you like him or what? He's a pretty radical guy.

> KATHY
> He is intense.

> SHERRIE
> Well?

> KATHY
> I am intrigued...

> CLINT
> 'nuff said!

INT. HUMANE SOCIETY - CLOSE UP ON KATHY

Simon is almost hidden in the corner quietly fascinated with the fish in the aquarium.

Kathy is lost in thought, petting a sleek, black kitty behind the customer counter.

> KATHY
> You're such a pretty kitty, aren't you, aren't you...

A male jerk walks into the room beaming with a crooked smile.

                    JERK
          That's right lady, that sure is
          some purrty kitty you got there.

When Simon hears Danny's voice coming in the front door, he straightens up quickly and without looking at him, tries to sneak out behind Danny unnoticed.

                    JERK (CONT'D)
          Hey, Simple Simon, what's shakin'?

                    SIMON
          Danny...

Simon ducks out the door quickly, virtually unscathed.

                    KATHY
               {Irritated}
          May I help you with something?

                    JERK
          Maybe so, 'cause a guy can't help
          just lookin' 'round, can he?

Kathy inattentively bends over to put the cat in its cage.

                    JERK (CONT'D)
          Mmm MMM! Nice kitty! Purty lady!

                    KATHY
               {Ignoring the comment}
          Now, what can I help you find
          today? A dog or a cat?

                    JERK
          How 'bout your phone number?

                    KATHY
          Fat chance on that, mister! You'll
          have to look somewhere else!

Surprised by Kathy's bluntness and mad at her instant rejection, Danny shakes his head.

                    JERK
          Didn't come lookin' for no dawg,
          that's for sure... If ya change yo
          mind...

The jerk walks out, sniffing around for another female to conquer. Kathy goes into the office where Paula is stationed.

KATHY
Men! I swear! There are jerks everywhere!

PAULA
You just need to find ya a good man. I'm waiting for a phone call from mine any minute now. Got him trained real good!

KATHY
I've had a hard time trusting men after my father left me.

PAULA
I thought he died? And died when you were just a girl?

KATHY
He did, but he still shouldn't have left me like that.

PAULA
Lordy, Lordy!

KATHY
{Chokes up} My mom couldn't feed both my sister and I so she ended up putting me in an orphanage.

Paula comes over beside Kathy, puts an arm around and pats her on the shoulder.

PAULA
Don't you worry your little heart out, sweetie, your mom didn't love your sister any more than she did you. She just had a very tough choice, tough, indeed!

KATHY
Ever since then, I had to fend for myself. I can't count the times I had to drive off a male staffer. Somehow, Lord knows how, I was more fortunate than the other girls, why...

Ringggg! The two make a mad dash for the phone. Paula beats Kathy to the counter.

                    PAULA
          {Warding off Kathy} Back off!!
          Hello, Humane Society.

Disappointment is on Paula's face. It's not her Sonny.
          ...Oh... yes... she's working right
          now...

Paula gives Kathy an irritated look.
          Looks like she just walked in. May
          I ask who is calling?... yes...

She thrusts the phone toward Kathy.
          {Whispers excitedly} It's Robert!

We hear Robert's voice through the phone Kathy is holding.

                    ROBERT
          You want to go for a sunset ride
          this weekend? We could go for a
          short ride, a long ride....

Fade out...

COUNTRY RIDE - MOTORCYCLE - KATHY AND ROBERT

We see the two riding on a winding highway through a thick forest. They stop and take a walk along trees sporting many ghostly beards of Spanish moss.

                    KATHY
          I love these ancient trees. Some of
          them have been here for hundreds of
          years!

                    ROBERT
          You are drawn to old things, are
          you?

                    KATHY
          I suppose. Mostly, I'm drawn to
          wisdom... things that stand the
          test of time... and beauty... the
          beauty here is timeless.

                    ROBERT
          Real beauty transcends time. Human
          forms don't last so long.

                    KATHY
          What is it about you?

ROBERT
What do you mean?

KATHY
Why am I asking you what I already know.

ROBERT
Know?

KATHY
You know things. I can feel that you do... feel?... I know you do.

ROBERT
How do you know me?

KATHY
I know you know. You are... wise, different... very powerful... {Grins} but very shy.

ROBERT
Shy?

KATHY
Mr. Penhaligon, If I were to take off all my clothes and jump into your arms, I don't think you'd know what to do.

ROBERT
{A little embarrassed}
You're right.

KATHY
Wow. There must be all of three of you on the planet.

The two stare at each other for a long moment.

KATHY (CONT'D)
How do you see the world?

ROBERT
It's One world. People don't see it as One. They like to divide and conquer. But it is One world. One world inside many...

KATHY
Why do we do that? Go to war, I mean?

ROBERT
Self deception. Death from the inside out. You get pollution... grief... It starts with the little things. Ego gratification at the cost of others. Conquest over unconditional love. Material pleasure over spiritual seeking.

KATHY
You put a cage around something long enough... it's hard... so hard.

ROBERT
{Sees Kathy getting upset}
Hey, you wanna ride further down to the ocean?

KATHY
{Relieved} Yeah, yeah. Let's go.

EXT. ISLE OF PALMS BEACH - OCEAN

The motorcycle is parked on the last edge of pavement.

KITARO's Agreement song is playing: "Watching the world from our window of life. Can we see all there is, that is real, that is right?"

Robert and Kathy race through the hot sand. Kathy is screaming in ecstacy as she suddenly stops at the cool wet line. Tentatively, she looks at the ocean, then at Robert.

KATHY (CONT'D)
I've never been to the ocean before!

ROBERT
It's okay! Run on in!

KATHY
Come with!

Kathy tugs off her jean shorts and is left wearing only a shimmering gold blouse that teasingly covers. Robert throws off his shirt and runs to catch up with Kathy as she runs further in. A wave crashes into her thighs and she hesitates at its power. Robert lightly chuckles.

ROBERT
Keep going! I'm here!

KITARO's Agreement still playing: "The fire, making me clean, making me fly, spinning me 'round, spinning me 'round!"

Kathy goes in DEEPER, braving each powerful wave. Suddenly she dives in and Robert dives in after her, intending to startle her by grasping for her legs which aren't there.

They both surface, laughing and breathless, five feet from each other. They make their way toward each other and hug and separate to dive several more times before Robert heads back to shore. Kathy is still ecstatic toward the power of waves.

KITARO's Agreement finishes: "This mystic time, I've known before, once before! The flame, within my heart, agreements made, are now realized, like before!"

As sunset approaches, the ocean comes alive in rainbow colors. Robert sees her full form as she emerges from the ocean. He becomes entranced with the sight of her and all of a sudden there is sunset fire in her eyes glowing at him! He flashes back on the water tower vision of a woman coming out of an ocean with her eyes on fire.

The wind comes up slightly in the last three minutes of The Beauty Of Time by STEVE MILLER. The song's gulls now cry.

      KATHY
  I didn't know this would be so
  amazing! There's nothing like this
  in Iowa!

      ROBERT
  {Astonished but laughing} I can't
  remember when I've had so much fun.

The Beauty Of Time's words rhythmically pour out: "We are children of the future" and repeats five more times.

Seven seagulls are gibbering around our couple's feet as they cautiously embrace. The gulls sound like the mud caked people wailing to the couple in the water tower vision.

ROBERT'S BEDROOM

Robert is in his bedroom and is staring at a tiny wisp of light flitting about.

      ROBERT
  I'm in trouble now...

He leans back on his bed and stares up at the ceiling.
  {Soft voice} Never thought it could
  feel so good.

EXT. STREET - DOWNTOWN AIKEN

Robert is walking down the busy street. He spots a young woman that looks like Kathy. Stunned, he follows hesitantly after her until he realizes she is indeed Kathy.
Hey! What do you know! Kathy!

KATHY
Robert! What are you doing here?

ROBERT
What do you mean, what am "I" doing here? You're on "my" street!

KATHY
Oh really? This is "your" town?

ROBERT
Well, I'm not against sharing... this time.

KATHY
{Hugs him} It's so good to see you!

Robert starts to beam as she continues:
Listen, do you have Memorial Day off?

ROBERT
Yeah.

KATHY
Would you like to go for a picnic?

ROBERT
Sure.

KATHY
I've heard of a great spot near the edge of town that sounds wonderful! I could bring some sandwiches.

ROBERT
Sure... and some deviled eggs, maybe? {He teasingly fishes}

EXT. MOTORCYCLE - HITCHCOCK WOODS

Kathy and Robert drive into Hitchcock woods. They stop at the edge of an open field and stroll, hand in hand, to the center. They sit down facing each other. By now clouds have gathered and melt together as one huge grayish white cloud. This does not seem to affect our couple lost in each other.

ROBERT (CONT'D)
{Looking around} It's been a long time since I've been here.

KATHY
{Breathless} It's beautiful!

ROBERT
Perhaps you'd like to try a contemplation with me out here in this special place.

KATHY
{In one sweet word around a silence that spoke years of mystery within her to explore} Okay.

ROBERT
I have a chant my ancestors passed down to me that I would like to share with you.

Still facing each other, they move into lotus positions. They chant softly in harmony. Some trees come alive by swaying gently in the breeze. After awhile, they fall silent. Off in the distance, the chant comes back through the trees and circles around them for a space.

MOODY BLUES song OM begins: "The Earth turns slowly round; Far away, the distant sound, is with us every day. Can you hear, what it says: Aum, Aum, Heaven!"

They open their eyes and look up. Directly overhead is a circular portal leading to the clear blue sky that was not there before. All else is cloud.

ROBERT (CONT'D)
Isn't nature so wonderful to connect with? So powerful?

Kathy nods.

KATHY
You are such a comfort to me. I feel I don't have to disguise my being with you. Your contact with me has been a gift I will always cherish.

ROBERT
I know you are a child of light. I can sense DEEPER things about you than with other women.

They move to lean against each other and play with each other's fingers. Lightening strikes close by. They watch the portal open even further right above them.

                   KATHY
     Who are you?

Robert only smiles.

                  KATHY (CONT'D)
     You are a magic man.

                  ROBERT
     Only because you are a magic woman.

He rubs his beard into her hair, gently laughing.

INT. KATHY'S LIVING ROOM - SPRING - 1973

Our couple snuggle together on a day-glow green love seat with bright flowery decals splashed all over it. In front of them, purple curtains are drawn away from the window. There is a used wooden cable reel pretending to be a dining table in the middle of the room. A peace symbol poster is tacked on the door. They are half whispering.

                  KATHY
     You remember the day we met?

                  ROBERT
     How could I forget?

                  KATHY
     The first time our eyes met, I'll
     never forget. I saw your third eye
     open. There was all this energy...

                  ROBERT
     You know the spiritual eye?

                  KATHY
     I've heard of it... but that was
     the first time I ever saw one... I
     also heard a voice just before
     falling asleep that same night.

                  ROBERT
     What did it say? {He reaches down
     to pick up a glass of iced tea}

                  KATHY
     To be with this man would be the
     most important decision of my life.

Robert brings the glass to his lips and then stops.

KATHY (CONT'D)
There will be responsibilities involved. If I chose to be with this man I would be crossing a doorway into something new.

Robert puts the glass down without drinking.

ROBERT
Did it say anything else?

KATHY
{Hesitating, she fibs} No.

ROBERT
I saw a vision of you when I was in high school and now it has come true. This is so fascinating! Both of us had some sort of Soul recognition.

KATHY
Oh, to see life all around us... even in the clouds. How can we not see magic?

ROBERT
Did you know that one and one make three?

KATHY
A man, a woman, and a child...

ROBERT
A man and a woman create a third entity unseen... When one sound approaches and interacts with another of a different pitch, they combine and produce a third sound, a harmonic, that is stronger and more vibrant than the two notes alone.

KATHY
You know what? {Toying voice}

ROBERT
What?

KATHY
You are the most beautiful man I've known!

                                    ROBERT
                        You're not so bad yourself!

They lean in for a first real kiss. A flash of lightning
lights up the room. Thunder booms loudly, then rolls off into
the distance.

                                    KATHY
                        Was that thunder inside us, or out
                        there?

                                    ROBERT
                        I saw the flash!

                                    KATHY
                        Your eyes were open? {She teases}

                                    ROBERT
                        No, ma'am!... Well, maybe just a
                        little!

They dash to the window. Not a single cloud is in the sky.
Their fate has been sealed by lightning. This is a marriage
made in Heaven.

Back on the love seat, they are caught up again in each
other's embraces. Multi-colored balls of light drift between
their eyes. The couple continue kissing and become more
passionate until Kathy loses control and starts tugging at
his shirt.

                                    ROBERT (CONT'D)
                        Wait a minute. Wait a minute! Let's
                        take our time.

                                    KATHY
                        Take our time! Rooobert!!!

                                    ROBERT
                        This is a special moment for us to
                        savor. Slowwwwly.

                                    KATHY
                        But I'm ready now!

                                    ROBERT
                        {Laughing} Come on, this would be
                        neat. A Tantric Milestone. Our
                        first time is the most important
                        time!... Our first time will never
                        happen again!

He can see his words slowly come as the most romantic she has
ever heard, and all meant for her. She softens.

KATHY
What do you have in mind?

ROBERT
Why don't we take off each other's clothes instead of our own?

KATHY
Okay.....

She starts grabbing at his clothes to rip them off. She has waited a long time for this and now these romantic words have her over the edge again.

ROBERT
No, not here on the love seat. Let's stand up.

Kathy becomes more and more intrigued as she is cooling down enough to do something like this. They move to the center of the room.

ROBERT (CONT'D)
Now wait! We are going to take off each other's clothes...

KATHY
{Interrupting} Yes...

She says this as she starts on him again but he stops her from grabbing.

ROBERT
...with our teeth...

She stops and looks at him like he is crazy.

KATHY
With our what? How?

ROBERT
I want us to take off each other's clothes using only our teeth.

KATHY
With our teeth?

ROBERT
Yes.

KATHY
That's impossible!

Kathy half wails, half trembles with delight.

                    ROBERT
          No, it's not! It's discipline! And
          we can't use our hands at all...
          Remember!

Kathy struggles with his top button using only her teeth.

                    KATHY
          Why didn't you wear a T-shirt
          today, of all days!

Her teeth are not cooperating the way she is hoping and the button just will not come off.

                    KATHY (CONT'D)
          I can't do it!

She is moaning and stamping her feet lightly.

                    KATHY (CONT'D)
          I can't wait to get my hands on
           you!

                    ROBERT
          No! No! No! No! Patience! Remember
          the rules. No hands!

He undoes the top button to insure she will not quit so soon. She struggles with the second button. Her head turns this way and that. Then her body even starts to look like a pretzel. Her hands are working on imaginary buttons in the air.

Pop!... Plunk!

The button bounces off the wall and hits the floor. His eyes roll toward the ceiling. A half-suppressed smile spreads across his face... She wails.

                    KATHY
          Ooh! I can't stand this any longer!

Robert groans at her not understanding he is trying to help her develop more patience. All the magic of the developing moment might slip away forever!

                    ROBERT
          We just started! Wait till it's my
          turn. You will love it!

This gives her something back she forgot about. Eager anticipation returns to her face. She manages to pull his shirt tail out. The bottom button comes undone with that action.

She absently places her hands on his hips as she concentrates on the last two buttons. He warns her, even though that feels sooo good.

ROBERT (CONT'D)
No hands at all!

KATHY
Oh!

She says this with a startled voice, as she pulls them off quickly. He makes a new suggestion.

ROBERT
Maybe it would be better if we clasp our hands behind our backs.

It works. She succeeds in pulling Robert's shirt off with her teeth. He decides to take a turn. He has no trouble with her blouse, but when it comes to her bra, he is embarrassed by not knowing how it clasps. She notices he doesn't have a clue and takes matters in her own hands, literally.

KATHY
Robert? Don't you know how a bra works?

ROBERT
I don't know how this one works.

KATHY
Robert! Tell me the truth!

ROBERT
I... um...

KATHY
Robert! You mean to tell me...

ROBERT
This is my first time...

KATHY
Robert! It's usually the other way around!

ROBERT
I was never interested in going DEEP with a woman... before you...

Her face turns to quiet sincerity. Another unexpected mystery with this man revealed. No wonder why he wants to make this Tantric. She unsnaps her bra but doesn't expect him to pull it off as slowly as he really does.

He gives her some love bites along the way. Her headlights come on. She has a far away look. She sighs.

>   KATHY
>   Not fair!

>   ROBERT
>   As long as I don't use my hands,
>   I'm legal!

It is her turn with his belt. Things are getting serious now. She settles into better concentration. A trick of the tongue and teeth and it is out of its loops. She has to walk around him several times to coax his jeans down, panting hard all the while.

He has his turn with much more control, but it is silently driving him wild to see her almost out of control. Moist lips travel curves, slowly teasing.

When all the clothes are gone, they continue standing there in the middle of the room. They move closer and slowly rub their bodies on each other. Both are breathing very regularly now.

After a few minutes of this they give into hands. Instead of eagerly ravishing to make up for lost time, they surprise themselves by slowly touching. Delicious moments.

Their knees grow weak in desire and they go down to a cross-legged position on the floor facing each other. She is sitting on his legs with her legs around his waist.

>   KATHY
>   Put it in.

She quietly breathes those words out, trembling all the while. What potent words to hear coming from her lips! He trembles in response.

>   ROBERT
>   Let's let it go in by itself.

They coax it slightly, but the idea is to move as little as possible, with as much restraint as possible, to allow for Tantric meditation.

They tremble for an hour, going in and out of ecstacy without climaxing. Sometimes they lose all desire and just drift free and comfortably in each other's arms. Not expecting, not pushing, just waiting for the inevitable to happen. Perhaps climax may not even come! Maybe there is a new goal waiting to be discovered. A spiritual one?

BLACK OAK ARKANSAS plays To Make Us What We Are: "To make you aware Magic is there, or do you care what we can share? Believe in Spirits, yes believe you're near it, we're on Earth to learn what Love is worth!"

Finally, without movement, but by trembling itself... What an explosion of energy! They rock and roll to it as if it would never end!

BLACK OAK: "Feel the Power a Saint can feel, then remember that you are Real. Let's be together, let's be as One, we'll shine as bright as any sun."

It is not one big explosion as expected. It is one explosion after another in rapid succession... And with each that would rock one partner, it transfers and rocks the other. They are so sensitive to each other's climaxes, that they are playing off each other.

INT. BEDROOM - KATHY AND ROBERT

Near dusk, we see the couple in bed. Between Robert's ecstatic breathing, we can hear Kathy's panting. Slowly, the two embrace and drop into sleep, exhausted.

Kaloom!

An eye half opens... then closes.

Ten seconds later...

Kaloom!...

The sound is bouncing all around. One eye fully opens, searching.

                    ROBERT (CONT'D)
    What's that sound?

Kathy awakens.

Kaloom!

                    KATHY
    I don't know.

Both heads are up. All eyes are searching.

                    ROBERT
    The clock's hands are reading seven
    sharp. But which seven? 7PM is dusk
    and 7AM is dawn? Which 7 are we?

Ten seconds later...

Kaloom!

> **KATHY**
> I think it's coming from the North.

A moment later...

Kaloom!

> **ROBERT**
> I think it's coming from the clock up there.
>
> **KATHY**
> Honey, I don't know. My clock never did that.
>
> **ROBERT**
> I never heard a clock do that.

Kaloom!

> **KATHY**
> Sounds like the clock slowed down.
>
> **ROBERT**
> You're not thinking what I'm thinking, are you?
>
> **KATHY**
> I think I am.
>
> **ROBERT**
> No, it can't be!
>
> **KATHY**
> Listen.
>
> **ROBERT**
> Shhh.

Kaloom.

> It sounds like the ticking second hand slowed down!
>
> **KATHY**
> It feels eerie in here.
>
> **ROBERT**
> Do you think time itself slowed down, Kathy?

                        KATHY
            Or maybe we sped up between time?

                        ROBERT
            Is it possible time is the same and
            we got caught between it?

                        KATHY
            It feels like the outside world is
            still going on and we are in some
            kind of time pocket.

Kaloom!

                        ROBERT
            It is coming from the clock. It IS
            a slow tick! And look at that! It
            is STILL seven o'clock!

They remain motionless, not wanting to break the spell, and just stare at each other. Suddenly!...

MONTAGE OF WORLD WIDE EMOTIONAL KARMA

Expanding shift of consciousness and they find themselves watching a parade of humans, some pontificating, some soaring in dance, others tirelessly pushing creaking carts up a hill. Mud sticks to their faces and arms. They chatter and squawk and sing in a clutter of world cultures. Some grapple others and curse.

A medicine man starts wailing as a minister pumps a holy book to the heavens. A happy baby gives a belly laugh.

7 balls of light appear before the couple and telepathically ask the couple, "Dooo yoou waant thee keeey {to this}?"

Kaloom!

Kathy and Robert are back in her bedroom together. A sharp intake of breath and they survey their surroundings.

Total silence. A floating calmness.

Kaloom!... And it is <u>still</u> seven o'clock!

Cloom... Cloom... cloom...

click... click... tick.

Tick tick, tick tick, tick tick, tick tick.

They find themselves back in regular time. Each minute contains a comfortable 120 ticks. The windows are getting darker. It is seven in the evening. Seven...

                KATHY
Wow.

                ROBERT
I wonder if anyone has died from too much of a good thing?

                KATHY
I think we have and went to Heaven.

                ROBERT
I see colors bursting out of my skin with your every touch.

                KATHY
I could lay here with you forever.

                ROBERT
You know, Camelot is not a physical location nor is it a mythical place. But it does exist! Camelot is a hidden place in the heart. A love like yours breaks all spells to make one free to return to Camelot.

                KATHY
You are my Arthur.

                ROBERT
And you are my Guinevere.

They kiss. Robert turns on the light.

                ROBERT (CONT'D)
I didn't realize how Tantric all this could be, sharing life. I have been alone all these years.

                KATHY
You come to me with pure love. It is so peaceful with a person on that level.

                ROBERT
All I know is that I love all that you are.

Another kiss.

KATHY
I am so very thankful that we have
finally met on the physical plane.
I have waited for you my lifetime.
This is a love so rare.

ROBERT
So magical.

Another kiss.

ROBERT (CONT'D)
You have brought so much fullness
into my life.

KATHY
Marry me.

The silence coming back at her was too much to bear.

KATHY (CONT'D)
I want to know you are mine
forever, Robert.

More profound silence and then he finally speaks.

ROBERT
I think it's too late.

Kathy freezes, almost afraid to ask.

KATHY
What do you mean?

ROBERT
I think we are already married...
the day we met, and now sealed with
lightning on the wings of a kiss!
We were brought together and
married in Heaven's eyes. No doubt!

KATHY
Let's make it official, then!

ROBERT
A Marriage made in Heaven is much
more important than a mundane
contract written on paper. How well
has THAT worked out for people?

More silence. Robert shifts his weight and gets up to find a couple of delicate stainless steel ball bearing chains from work and offers one to her.

He wraps one in three loops which fits perfectly on his left ankle. He wraps the other in three loops also, but around her right ankle.

> ROBERT (CONT'D)
> We are bonded together! Your right ankle signifies the masculine, your connection to me. My left ankle signifies the feminine, my connection to you. May our sacred bond never be broken! Now it is official!

With tears of joy in her eyes, she pulls him back to the bed and on top of her.

> KATHY
> I love you, Roberrt! {Lilting his name}

EXT. HITCHHIKING - COAST TO COAST - SUMMER - 1973

Robert and Kathy are hitchhiking across the States.

Song in the background is THE FLOWERPOT MEN: "Let's go to San Francisco where the flowers grow so very high. Sunshine in San Francisco makes your mind grow up to the sky. Lots of sunny people... they have found their land."

The St. Louis arch passes by the window, blending with other sights as they travel the States. Fade out...

Our couple have been stranded on the Salt Lake City exit ramp most of the day. Other thumbers are first by the rules of the road. It is a hot day. Robert finally shows disappointment.

> ROBERT
> Oh, man! We will never get our turn today!

Kathy makes a strange announcement.

> KATHY
> We are going to be picked up! Not only that, but in this heat it will be by a cool black Cadillac!

Robert chuckles and shakes his head but won't bring her back to reality. He thinks to himself, "Dream on."

Fifteen minutes later, they are picked up by a pretty young woman in a black air conditioned Cadillac. She accelerates to cruise at 95 MPH across miles and miles of boring sand flats.

A motorcycle policeman stops them. The driver is trying to flirt her way out of a ticket. She gets out to show him her fake concern about her tires. Her long black hair is blowing in the wind. As she bends over to point, her short billowy dress blows up to reveal no panties! Ticket problem resolved! Onward, the youngsters travel, carefree and excited!

Song playing in the background is SCOTT McKENZIE's "If you're going to San Francisco, be sure to wear some flowers in your hair... All across the Nation, such a strange vibration. People in motion. There's a whole generation with a new explanation. People in motion. People in motion."

We see our couple jumping off a rusty old pickup in front of an ashram in San Francisco. They join the meditators in progress. Flash to another ashram and yet another as the couple join meditation activities and talk to people.

Eventually they go through the Golden Gate Bridge by bus and get to San Rafael. They are a little shaken by the sanitary upscale city in contrast with the mean streets of San Francisco.

INT. OFFICE OF KUNDALINI ASHRAM - SAN RAFAEL

>   SAT SANTOCK
> I am pleased to hear you want to join our Ashram! I think you would just love it here. The Kundalini training is excellent! You can train anywhere from one hour to six hours a day with various groups.

>   ROBERT
> But how can we pay for this? We don't have much...

>   SAT SANTOCK
> Your toil in the marvelous gardens and maintenance of the buildings will pay your room and board. And we have one great family here! I was the road manager for the Grateful Dead before coming here which qualified me to keep this place on task while the main Guru is away. We have private rooms for couples, we have rooms for men only and rooms for women only. Are you guys married or not?

                    ROBERT
          Why? Does that make any kind of
          difference?

Both Kathy and Sat Santock are affirming to a stunned Robert at the same time and Sat finishes with:

                    SAT SANTOCK
          Well, you two have to be married to
          be able to share a couple's room.

                    ROBERT
          What? Are you kidding?

Sat has a very determined look on his face.

                    ROBERT (CONT'D)
          Can't we just stay a couple of
          weeks first to see what we think?

                    SAT SANTOCK
          If you don't mind sleeping in
          different rooms.

                    ROBERT
          Fine with me. Let's try that Kathy.

                    KATHY
          I am not going to do that again! I
          didn't like being separated from
          Mark, and it will be even worse
          this time without you next to me.

                    ROBERT
          {Surprised} Are you sure?

Kathy shakes her head emphatically. Robert looks back to Sat.

                    ROBERT (CONT'D)
          Well, we don't have the
          conventional piece of paper. We are
          married by the Holy Spirit and that
          is WAY more important than a stupid
          piece of paper written up by stupid
          lawyers. What do they know about
          real love? Nothing!

                    SAT SANTOCK
          I agree with you 100 percent!
          Believe me! But unfortunately this
          Ashram is one of the three Ashrams
          in the States in which the Head
          Guru comes to stay and we never
          know when he is going to appear.

This news causes a quick debate between Kathy and Robert considering to marry or not. Sat mentions being licensed to perform weddings. Kathy is excited at this news. Idealistic Robert decides a firm "no" to a mundane marriage. Kathy is sad. A profound shift of Destiny is felt by both. They leave and find an apartment in Berkeley.

INT. BERKELEY APARTMENT

          ROBERT
So what do you think?

          KATHY
        {Looking around}
I like it.

          ROBERT
Well, good, because we can get it.

          KATHY
You're kidding!

          ROBERT
Nope. We got enough to cover a couple of months.

          KATHY
Great! Let's take it! Let's take it! {Laughs and hugs him}

EXT. EAGLE - TILDEN PARK - BERKELEY

A golden eagle soars effortlessly over the forest and spies Robert leaning against a tree and Kathy leaning against him. The eagle perches on top of a huge redwood tree. Both trees are swaying in a gentle breeze. It was as if all were connected to each other by the breeze.

          KATHY
I feel as if we have been here before. It's all so familiar.

          ROBERT
It is so beautiful, isn't it? It is so peaceful up here.

          KATHY
It's like Deja Vu! This tree I know and that rock formation up there. I knew it was up there before we came up to it!
            (MORE)

KATHY (CONT'D)
All of this is so familiar, the way
we touch and move with the tree. I
knew what you were going to say
before you said it.

ROBERT
When I feel this way I marvel that
I visited the future in a dream
half-remembered. It feels like an
Eternal Moment captured in the Now.

The couple embrace and then sit cross-legged, knees touching each other. They take a few DEEP breaths then begin to hum into a soft chant. Some of Berkeley is peeping out from the trees below. The Bay water is shimmering sunlight back up to the couple. Kathy looks DEEPLY into Robert's eyes.

KATHY
Tell me your secret, Magic Man.

ROBERT
You are a Magic Woman.

Suddenly we hear the lone cry of a coyote... It is answered by another call and then the two merge into a haunting cry that drifts and undulates around them.

ROBERT (CONT'D)
To see the world in a grain of sand
and a heaven in a wild flower, hold
infinity in the palm of your hand
and eternity in an hour.

KATHY
That is beautiful. Is it yours?

ROBERT
William Blake, an eighteenth
century visionary. I have been
reading of him in the West Berkeley
library.

KATHY
I love you.

ROBERT
We are one. Irretrievably merged.
Being with you makes the world more
open and accessible somehow... I am
learning what it means to love and
be loved.

Kathy reaches up and caresses Robert's cheek.

                    KATHY
          Do you really love ME?

                    ROBERT
          Of course I do! What makes you ask
          that?

                    KATHY
          I just want to hear you say it more
          often.

                    ROBERT
          I am sorry. I feel it so palpably
          every day with you, it seems there
          is no need to go as far as
          verbalizing it.

                    KATHY
          Will you marry me some day?

                    ROBERT
          Kathy..... we... are...

They both look DEEPLY into each other's eyes.

                    KATHY
          I've noticed some people who
          normally seem so much in control of
          their lives, become uncomfortable
          under your gaze. What is that about
           you?

                    ROBERT
          I don't know. I can't help but
          really look at people. Eyes connect
          truth beyond mere words.

                    KATHY
          You remember Paula from the Humane
          Society? She felt so uncomfortable,
          she once told me she thought your
          eyes were dangerous eyes.

                    ROBERT
          I don't mean to do that.

THE MOODY BLUES song Have You Heard is playing: "Now you know
that you are real."

                    KATHY
          I just see love in your eyes.

The couple stare longer until a tiny rainbow appears and
bridges between their eyes.

                        KATHY (CONT'D)
    Oh my!!!

MOODY BLUES... "Show your friends that you and me, belong to the same world, turned on by the same word, have you heard?"

INT. INNER VISION SEQUENCE

We see our couple in the Old West. She is a long black haired Native-American. He is a white bearded mountain man. They gaze into each other's eyes.

Shift into seventeenth century France. She is his wife. They have two beautiful little girls. Eyes meet. They embrace.

MOODY BLUES... "Each day has its Always, a look down life's hallways, doorways, to lead you there."

Shift to fourteenth century Italy. They are a young couple resisting an inevitable separation. Sad eyes. Bells ring in the background for him to take monastic vows.

Shift behind the scenes of a Roman gladiator training ground. They are both men, their eyes meet in sympathy as Robert dies at a brute's big body crushing him into the gallery bars.

Shift to time of the Vikings. Both have long knotty locks of hair. Shift to Ancient Celts. He sees her face cheering him into battle.

Shift to Ancient Brittany. The couple is seen playful outside an idyllic homestead setting.

Shift to Ancient Egypt. Robert is being entombed and she is one of three handmaidens being buried in the same Immortal Chamber.

MOODY BLUES... "Life's ours for the making, Eternity's waiting, waiting, for you and me. Have you heard? Have you heard? Have you heard?"

Shift to Ancient Lemuria and the couple lock eyes. Shift to travelling into DEEP space and we see the couple together in the Maia system of the Pleiades.

Fade out...

INT. BERKELEY APT - NIGHT

Robert is in bed. Kathy is laying on top Robert. She is toying with his beard in the semi-darkness.

                    KATHY
          I can scarcely believe that
          happened.

                    ROBERT
          What's that, my angel?

                    KATHY
          Seeing our past lives together.

                    ROBERT
          Looks like all this Kundalini has
          paid off... ashram or no ashram.

                    KATHY
          I never experienced anything like
          this.

                    ROBERT
          I think it is also the magic of our
          bond beyond human understanding.

                    KATHY
          It's too real! Too incredible. No
          one would believe this!

                    ROBERT
          But here we are! And who's to say
          if these vivid memories are really
          our past lives? The most important
          thing is: What is the lesson?

They kiss. A slight glow is seen around the couple's heads.
They spoon and fall asleep.

DREAMSCAPE

Robert is floating upright in the clouds. Kathy appears
through the clouds and stops within 5 feet of Robert.

                    KATHY
          I am yours.

Robert takes her hand and they fly up through the clouds and
into DEEP space. They stop to look back and see our galaxy in
the distance. Robert becomes excited.

                    ROBERT
          They knew! The Ancient Ones knew
          all along!
                         (MORE)

                    ROBERT (CONT'D)
          They not only travelled into the
          Microcosm and left Ancient Sanskrit
          texts describing the makeup of an
          atom, but they travelled out here
          into the Macrocosm and saw our
          dance of Duality!

Robert points a finger.
          Look! Our galaxy is what inspired
          their Yin/Yang symbol!

                    KATHY
          I see the whole universe! Yet, I
          understand more than I can see. I
          know that Soul is formless yet
          never lacks a form. The physical
          body is frozen thought in all its
          shapes and sizes.

Our couple look into each other's eyes. Balls of light 3" in diameter float around them. They smile with understanding.

                    ROBERT
          Do you feel this, too? Are you here
          with me?

                    KATHY
          Yes!

Robert and Kathy both snap awake in bed facing each other.

                    ROBERT
          Did you say "Yes"?

                    KATHY
          Yes!

EXT. STREETS OF BERKELEY

Robert is seen being turned down for a job. Kathy is 2 blocks away and being propositioned to pose nude for photographs in exchange for money. She turns him down.

Robert is seen walking down San Pablo street and bumps shoulders with a high class stripper getting out of a Caddy. She is the epitome of beauty but her nose is red and her eyes look pained. Powerful silence. No words are exchanged. She locks eyes with his compassion and is taken momentarily. She recovers and continues toward a discotheque.

Robert walks on and finds Kathy.

INT. BERKELEY APARTMENT

      KATHY (CONT'D)
 I can't believe you turned down
 that job!

Kathy is visibly upset. She stands in place in the kitchen looking like she wants to go in two directions at once. Robert is in the dining room.

      ROBERT
 What job?

      KATHY
 That job at the gas station.

She breaks free to pace the kitchen.

      ROBERT
 What job at what gas station?

      KATHY
 Don't act innocent with me! You
 said it was beneath you and now
 look where we're at!

One at a time, she slams all the kitchen cabinets to get her point across. There is nothing to eat.

      ROBERT
 Oh, <u>that</u> gas station!

      KATHY
 Oh, <u>that</u> gas station! Of course
 that gas station! What else except
 that gas station?

      ROBERT
 I didn't turn down any job at that
 gas station.

      KATHY
 Okay, what would you say it was,
 then?

      ROBERT
 {Hurt from being misunderstood}
 I told you, because of the recent
 shoot out there, I wasn't even
 <u>going</u> to consider asking for a job
 there. That was the third shooting
 they had recently and they weren't
 even offering any jobs anyway. I,
 didn't turn down any <u>job</u>!

KATHY
Well, what about the motorcycle shop?

ROBERT
I've been in there multiple times and they just aren't hiring.

KATHY
Maybe if you'd cut your hair like the emergency aid lady said.

Kathy throws herself onto the living-room couch.

ROBERT
That's a low blow.

KATHY
I know, but dammit, Robert, we deserve better than this! The point is: one sacrifice for another. Do you pick hair over food?

ROBERT
It's my choice and my freedom to live how I want to be. I can't allow some uptight square to dictate how I should wear my hair! Besides, these places are telling me that the college students have taken all the available summer jobs. And many of them have long hair. It's Berkeley! Smack dab in the era of love!

Robert sits down on the couch close to her and tries to hold her. She resists.

ROBERT (CONT'D)
Remember the stripper I saw? She was so beautiful, but when I was close enough to see her eyes, I saw her pain. I will never forget that look. The broken dreams. The shattered love pushed down so DEEP within her. She walked bravely into that discotheque. The last shreds of that love to be murdered by her own hand. She knew she wouldn't be able to kill it all, but she would still try. That pained me DEEPLY.

KATHY
Your point being, Mr. Penhaligon?

ROBERT
My point being, I don't want either one of us to prostitute ourselves for money.

KATHY
Or compromise our harebrained ideals?

ROBERT
Not harebrained. Maybe... stubborn. But we will move out of state if we must. I have friends in Denver.

Robert pulls the rigid curve of her body to himself. Kathy relaxes into his arms.

KATHY
I miss you talking like that.

ROBERT
I know.

KATHY
I'm sorry what I said about your hair. You groom it well even if your beard is a little shaggy.

She gives his beard a little love tug.

KATHY (CONT'D)
I love it. I love you the way you are.

ROBERT
I wouldn't have anyone but you. I was fortunate to find you.

Robert kisses her neck.

KATHY
What do you mean *you* found *me*?

She throws him back on the couch, pressing her body to his and kissing him.

MONTAGE: STREET VIOLENCE - BERKELEY

Assaults on the streets in the daylight. Burglary at night time. The parking garage is set on fire below them. Patty Hearst is kidnapped by SLA and seen robbing a bank.

FADE TO:

Kathy and Robert on a Freak Bus {Greyhound converted for hippie travel} leaving Berkeley and passing into Denver.

INT. CONCRETE JUNGLE - BOULDER

Robert is drafting for an electronics firm. Fade to Kathy working in a book store. Busy, busy, busy, stress.

Fade to Kathy and Robert eating in a restaurant with Mike and Ginger. The same Mike from Aiken Elementary School, but now with a cool handlebar moustache, reminding one of a young, casual Burt Reynolds, always up to something with that smile.

Buds forever! Now they like riding motorcycles together everywhere! The four of them travel through the mountains on weekends. Two couples, two bikes, too much fun... not.

EXT. RUSH HOUR - BOULDER - EARLY SEPT. MORNING - 1974

Robert is on a street-chopped 650 Yamaha with extended handlebars. Extended front forks. Custom extended exhaust pipes up in position to double as a sissy bar. He is on his way to work. The sun is coming up behind him.

SHAWN PHILLIP'S Early Morning Hours playing: "And when the Light comes down to guide me, I will not bow down and hide me, no siree, respectfully. And it is better to be humble than pontificate and bumble through the spree, of the people tree. And like the Martlet of the Legend, I am on my way to Heaven, if I do not touch the ground, I'll make it home..."

A white Toyota coming the opposite direction, crosses the median. They collide. Robert is thrown through the extended handlebars and into the air in slow motion. The motorcycle crumples below him. The extended exhaust pipes break off at seat level and go flying 80+ feet into a parking lot.

Robert splits in two. His physical body turns one complete flip, lands on his feet and crumples to the ground unconscious. His Soul body stays suspended in the air and is surrounded by a grey cloud.

                    ROBERT
    {Relieved} That's it! It's over! I
    must have finished early all I was
    supposed to do on Earth! 24 not 34?

A thunderous peal sounding like a thousand jets rippling across the sky descends upon him as a large rainbow-colored tunnel. His Soul body is drawn upward through it.

Robert holds out his left hand. A Golden Ring appears in his palm, upright and spinning. {A Golden Meh from Father Enki?} A DEEP resonant voice comes forth from the Ring. Robert's gaze is held, entranced by it.

>   DEEP RING VOICE
>   Whooo arrre yooou?

>   ROBERT
>   I am Robert.

>   DEEP RING VOICE
>   Heerre iss my beloved son, Roberrt!

Sequential scenes from Robert's past flash before him as he travels further up the tunnel. It ends with Robert's body being shot by four body guards of a top leader for Yogi Bhajan, jealous of Robert's swift attainment.

Sat Santock and Kathy are seen crying over his dead body in the potential future of 1984 changed. The seemingly minor decisions in life... documented marriage, or no documented marriage.

EXT. HOSPITAL

Robert is seen being taken out of an ambulance on a gurney by the emergency crew. They roll him to the hospital door.

Inside shot of three double doors being banged by the gurney as they travel through. Robert's head is at the lead edge of the gurney taking the blows. He appears unconscious.

INT. BOOKSTORE - BOULDER

>   KATHY
>   What are you doing here, Ginger?

>   GINGER
>   It's Robert! He has been in an
>   accident!

>   KATHY
>   What are you talking about?

>   GINGER
>   Come on! Let me take you to the
>   hospital!

>   KATHY
>   How bad is it?

HEAVEN

Robert's Soul body comes out of the top of the tunnel floating in the sky above a pastoral scene. The greenery below is spotted with white gazebos and scattered white pillars. The background sound is a full rich "Huuu" of a thousand DEEP voices.

Robert floats up the side of a mountain. A white glowing temple is seen at the top. He continues floating up to meet the top of the temple. He is seen disappearing into an opening almost 3/4 of the way up the side of the rounded spire of the temple.

INT. HEAVENLY TEMPLE

The glowing alabaster walls themselves are resounding the "Huuu" as if they are alive also. Inside are vast archways and alabaster-like pillars reaching up into a high vaulted dome. Everything is white. The pillars and walls are opaque and glowing from the inside. Corridors can be seen leading to other chambers. Robert is led floating inches above the floor into another chamber.

Inside, Robert sees many rows of long benches. There are several work tables off to one side. As he is led past each row of benches, he can see graduation years stamped at each row. Invisible entities sit in rows that don't concern him. As he passes the one stamped "1968" he can see Danny, Mike, Simon and other familiar faces bonded by karma.

                    DEEP RING VOICE
          These are places people come to in
          their sleep to learn what may
          become of them if they continue on
          their present course. They are
          permitted to remember just a few
          images upon waking.

INT. HOSPITAL

Shot from far up looking down as if right through the ceiling, Robert is seen with eyes closed in a hospital bed. All is silent except for a slight angelic musical chorus.

INT. MOVING CAR

Ginger is driving. Kathy is seated next to her, weeping.

                    KATHY
          What else did the nurse say?

>   GINGER
>   She just told me to get you here as
>   soon as possible.
>
>   KATHY
>   My God! That's not fair!
>   Don't let him die!
>
>   GINGER
>   We are almost there, Kathy!
>   Hold on!

INT. HEAVENLY TEMPLE

Robert's Soul is led into another corridor. The main chamber is in his sight and is glowing even more than the other places. The source of the resonant "Huuu" sound appears to be from this chamber. DEEP Full Compassionate Love is felt here {Musical enrichment}. A memory flashes of Robert at age 11 falling out of a swing and feeling this same peace and love.

As Robert enters the chamber, the Ring leaves his hand. There are Seven Beings of Light standing behind a stretch lectern side by side. The tallest being is in the middle, and seems to radiate Great Compassion. All Seven are in perfect symmetry to each other.

All Seven are mostly light, including halos, but human features can be seen in each face. There are also strands of light weaving between them like they are all tied together, yet each Being is distinct and separate. Each seem to have a different dominant Virtue radiating outward prism-like from the Center Being, through them and out to All Mankind.

The Golden Ring spins over to and above the halo of the center Being {Father Enki?} and hovers in the shaft of light that is pouring down on him.

Robert is now standing in front of the Seven Beings of Light. There are benches seen behind him. Are these the Biblical Seven Flames Before The Throne? Are these The Seven Pre-Sumerian Anunnaki Who Decree From Heaven And Judge In Hell? Seven Above? Seven Below?

>   ROBERT
>   You know who I am. Who are you?

The Seven Beings speak of one accord inside Robert's head. They powerfully throw his words back on him.

>   SEVEN BEINGS
>   Huuu Arre Youuuuu?

Images of the world's past appear in Robert's Mind. When the present is reached, the landscape opens into a panoramic view and Robert's Soul is placed right down in the center of it. Robert is in the middle of war and suffering and famine on a large scale. Robert flinches in horror as the bloody realistic scenes continue one after another.

>ROBERT
>How can this be?

>SEVEN BEINGS
>Theeese arrre the probable future events of your planet. Every <u>thing</u> is in flux. Every <u>one</u> isss tied together in thisss.

The Gulf War is shown. The Twin Towers. The beginning invasion into Iraq {Camels following tanks}. Japan's 9.0 earthquake and tsunami. California's coming 9.3+ earthquake. Alaska/Seattle's coming 9.5+ earthquake. The Ring of Fire.

>ROBERT
>Flux? Probable reality? I want the Ultimate Truth! Ultimate Reality!

The future visions melt away in obeyance to his request.

>SEVEN BEINGS
>Inn goood tiimme, My Sonnn.

An incredible future vision appears of Robert in 2034.

>ROBERT
>But you promised me I could stay here! I don't need to go back!

>SEVEN BEINGS
>Youuu Musst Returrrrn!

>ROBERT
>No!!!

INT. HOSPITAL

Vague visibility. A heart monitor is heard very weakly. The scene comes into view, and we see Robert in a hospital bed and Kathy is leaning over it, holding his arm. Ginger is close by. The heart monitor speeds up and Robert jolts to consciousness.

>ROBERT
>No! You promised me!

                    KATHY
          Robert! You are awake! You are here
          with us. Thank God!

                    ROBERT
          The Ashram! Why am I not dead?

                    KATHY
          Robert. You are here in the
          hospital. You are all right.

                    ROBERT
          The hospital? Is this real?

                    GINGER
          Yes, we are real. Welcome back! We
          were so worried for you...

                    ROBERT
          This can't be real! Where I was, is
          more real than this!

                    KATHY
          What are you talking...

A nurse comes running in and resets the monitor alarm.

                    NURSE
          Mr. Penhaligon, you are awake!
          Good! The doctors have been hoping
          to talk with you. How you didn't
          break both legs going through those
          handlebars is beyond me! We have
          never seen anyone so lucky on a
          motorcycle before in the history of
          this hospital!

Robert smiles at this news and asks:

                    ROBERT
          Where is my bike?

                    NURSE
          Impound, I imagine. The towing
          company reported that parts of your
          motorcycle were found 120 feet away
          from the accident itself.

Robert remembers three warning dreams in the past month of
his extended exhaust pipes snapping off. Eerie, but a lot of
good that did him! He couldn't stop it from really happening!

                    ROBERT
          My pipes... My exhaust pipes...

> NURSE
> How did you know?

He keeps this to himself... except for Kathy, later.

INT. ROBERT AND KATHY'S LIVINGROOM - NIGHT

A magic carpet is in the middle of the floor. Robert is sitting lotus style on the floor as best he can with a cast on his left foot. He is staring out the window. In full view, scanning from right to left are two street lights glowing, a billboard, then five more street lights. He is staring at the far right street light and it goes out. He stares at the next one to the left and it goes out. The billboard is sideways to the window but fully facing the road. It is lit by eight flood lights below it in the frame. He stares at the billboard and it goes dark with an audible bang.

Kathy walks into the livingroom.

> KATHY
> You've changed since the accident.

> ROBERT
> It's the pain.

> KATHY
> Your ankle? Or is your back flaring up again? Why the heck you didn't let the doctors fuse your fractured spine is beyond me!

> ROBERT
> No. World pain. How can people be so cruel to each other? They're even cruel to themselves. Don't they know that the future is in their own hands?

> KATHY
> Robert, let's not go there again.

> ROBERT
> And then there is this... Look...

Robert points his finger at the first light to the left of the billboard. He is concentrating on it.

> KATHY
> What happened to the billboard?

The light Robert points at goes out. He points at the next to the left and it goes out. Points, another out.

Now, without the excess light pollution, Orion and Gemini can be seen clearly in the sky. A meteor shoots between the two.

> KATHY (CONT'D)
> What's next, my Magic Man?

Robert shifts his body so his right shoulder is facing the window. Kathy sits down, lotus style, to face him. The couple smile and stare into each other's eyes. A rainbow arcs in from the window and lands between the couple. We can hear them both breathing DEEPLY.

RARE BIRD's 1970 As Your Mind Flies By plays: "Flowing rivers, craggy mountains sigh. Wondering, watching as your mind flies by.... Now's the time to free your mind, fly, fly, fly."

One and then another 1/2" diameter glowing balls come out from Robert's forehead and float towards Kathy's forehead. Several are seen passing back and forth for a short time.

> ROBERT
> {Suddenly, almost painfully}
> Ahh!

Shot from behind Robert, we see a column of light moving up his spine.

> ROBERT (CONT'D)
> I can't stop!

The column of light moves up into his head making his head glow. Then we see two transparent, white DNA cobras wrapping around his lower spine, moving up and both coming out the sides of his neck to rest just above his shoulders.

RARE BIRD continues: "Hold your head up to the sky, fly high. See the Heavens open doors, fly by. Angels hold you near, now your path is clear, God has cast out fear, mind fly by."

A three inch ball of rainbow light comes out the top of his head. It moves toward the ceiling. Another rainbow from the window joins it. The ball of light drops into the top of Kathy's head. The serpents and the spinal glow subside, but now Kathy and Robert are glowing slightly.

A sigh comes from one or maybe both of them and they slump forward until their foreheads touch. Their hair is crackling with electricity. He is telepathic like everyone was in the Heavenly journey. She responds audibly.

> KATHY
> Yes, I hear you.

Our couple slump over to their sides and embrace. Their molecules are speeding up. Robert's hand appears to be merging into Kathy's side. He pulls away, a little startled. Kathy places a hand on his chest and it sinks in just to his heart. They both look at each other, astonished. We can hear the couple next door start to argue.

> ROBERT
> You know them... They won't stop once they get started.

Robert hobbles over to the livingroom wall. He looks back at Kathy and looks back to the wall. He holds his hand out like a stop sign and hesitates. He slowly lowers his arm until his finger tips are just touching the wall. Then his arm passes through the wall into the arguing couple's livingroom. The couple stop arguing. {They quietly move out in four days.}

Robert smiles, shakes his head and moves back to position with Kathy. If the choice had been made to stay in the Ashram, the jealous Yogi would have had Robert killed for antics like this. Our couple close their eyes and become motionless.

INT. LANDSCAPE OF A DREAM - MOMENTS LATER

RARE BIRD finishes: "Cast yourself and sail into the sun, you've had your fun. Now your time has come. Now your time has come. Now your Time has Come."

Robert and Kathy are seen standing on the summit of Mount Shasta, a majestic 14,162 feet. A rainbow of light is seen around the curve of the planet like a natural aura.

Time speeds up. The sun sets as the moon comes up, three times its normal size like a Supermoon, and glowing orange.

The couple spy another majestic peak in the distance. The moonlit snow sparkles like jewels. The couple fly off in that direction.

FADE OUT INTO ANOTHER DREAMSCAPE

The couple is seen landing at 29,028 feet, on the summit of Sagarmatha, sacred Everest. Pre-dawn light of another day.

The couple survey the landscape. A flock of geese are pushing upward in the currents below, attempting the pass. The calm, distinct low hum of the Earth can be heard.

A brilliant point of light comes out of the sky and grows larger as it reaches within 150 feet of the couple.

It slows and breaks off into Seven distinct lights. A DEEP resonant "Huuu" is being heard.

As the lights approach, the "HUUU" is richer and stronger. The Seven from Heaven hover at 40 feet above the couple.

> SEVEN BEINGS
> Immortal, yooou have broken the Seal of Deatthh... Gooo... Tell others, "You may visit the Heavens beforrre the body diieess."

FADE OUT as Thunder from different directions play together in the skies, just as crickets throw their songs to each other in the fields. It is all Beautifully interwoven.

INT. BOOKSTORE - BOULDER - 1975

Shirley is cashing out a customer. Jon, from the men's clothing store down the Mall's hallway, walks into the bookstore with Kathy. They are both holding cups.

> KATHY
> Thanks for the soda, Jon.

Jon holds up his cup in salute.

> KATHY (CONT'D)
> But you know I can't go out drinking and partying with you.

> JON
> No harm in asking.

> KATHY
> You know I'm a married woman.

> JON
> I've told you he's no good for you. Give me a call when you tire of him. I will be here for you.

> KATHY
> Yeah, sure. See you later, Jon.

> JON
> Hustle some good business today.

Jon salutes her and Shirley with his cup. Shirley waves him off with a smile. How charming he seems!

Jon walks down the hall towards the men's clothing store, sniffing around for more eye candy. You wait, you lose!

SHIRLEY
Jon's a pretty nice guy. I kept an eye on him since before he became manager of that clothing store.

KATHY
So that's what makes him so cocky. I kind of like that.

SHIRLEY
Between you and I, I think he snorts some white lines. He's quite a social animal, you know.

KATHY
I know! The fast lane is beginning to look pretty exciting.

SHIRLEY
It's a crazy world.

KATHY
I've met some pretty interesting characters while working here. It's kind of opened my eyes to change.

INT. KATHY'S DREAM

Robert and Kathy are sitting together on chairs with a small table between them. All else is cloud. Robert is reading to Kathy from his Antahkarana. Kathy is nodding off.

ROBERT
Pray help me slip behind the veil once more!
I gaze to catch glimpses of connections DEEP.
With all united, preternatural patterns will steep.
Things once plain, open as flowers and reveal their inner core...

KATHY
{Head jerks slightly} Robert, I can't stay awake.

ROBERT
I can help you stay awake... Wake up, wake up!

INT. BOOKSTORE - STORAGE ROOM

Kathy wakes up and sees that she is sitting at the same table but Robert is not there. Kathy had fallen asleep while on break. The manager enters the back room.

                    SHIRLEY
          Kathy, Ginger is here.

Kathy gets up and heads for the door.

                    KATHY
          Thanks, Shirley. I will be back
          after lunch.

INT. MALL - COMMON AREA

Kathy and Ginger are sitting in chairs, sipping soft drinks.

                    GINGER
          Yes, Kathy. Mike and I have known
          Robert years before you came along
          and stole his heart. You are his
          first love.

                    KATHY
          So you, of anyone, would know if he
          seems different.

Ginger laughs.

                    GINGER
          Well, he has always been a little
          different than others... but in a
          sweet way.

                    KATHY
          No, I mean different from how he
          used to be.

                    GINGER
          Well, he's always been sort of
          innocent and blunt at the same
          time... Let me correct that
          statement... Disarmingly honest.

They both smile. Then Kathy's brows become knitted. She speaks somewhat hesitantly.

                          KATHY
            I don't mean to sound weird or
            anything, Ginger, but he has had
            some kind of explosion of
            consciousness since his motorcycle
            was totaled. He died! He was dead!

Ginger waits for more.

                          KATHY (CONT'D)
            I don't know! He can just do
            things, that...

Kathy trails off while Ginger stares at her inquisitively.

                          KATHY (CONT'D)
            I don't know. He takes me places
            where I have never been. No one has
            been! Aren't these forbidden lands?

Kathy looks at her watch and stands up.

                          GINGER
            {Smiles} Is that a bad thing?

Kathy's floodgate opens as she paces back and forth. Ginger jumps up and attempts to hold her.

                          KATHY
            It scares me a little. I love him
            so much but I can't keep up with
            him. When we touch, it is like our
            energy explodes. I like it but then
            it really gets intense, almost out
            of control. When we make love, it
            is like he is making love to the
            whole Universe, not just with me.

Ginger is hugging Kathy. Kathy is now sobbing in Ginger's shoulder.

                          KATHY (CONT'D)
            It's like the Steiner book Zanoni
            come alive. I never would have
            believed it before now. Either my
            nature must be lifted up to
            Robert's or his nature must be
            drawn down to mine. I can't do that
            to him. I can't limit him! I can't!

Meanwhile Ginger is whispering.

                          GINGER
            There, there, Kathy. Shh. Shh.

                        KATHY
            No one can go with him... No one...

INT. ROBERT'S BOOK ROOM

Robert is seated on the floor in lotus position with no cast on his foot. Eyes closed. Three philosophy books surround him on the floor. He is talking to himself out loud with pauses between words as they come to him out of the blue.

                        ROBERT
            Complete confrontation with oneself
            leads to truth. The price of truth
            is any and every pain and joy
            brought forth for investigation.

At that moment a beam of white light penetrates the ceiling, striking Robert, pulsing through him, scatters across the floor in all directions wild, gathering up and leaving out the window like bright daylight being sucked out into space. His body tingles. The roar of a waterfall when the light passed through now turns to the DEEP familiar thunderous rippling we have come to know.

A figure stands before Robert in the room. It toys with its long beard. A red rose is in its right hand. This figure, and all the ones to come, speak in inhumanly DEEP voices from out the matrix of the background "Huuu."

                        BLAKE
            Whooo ammm IIII?

                        ROBERT
            William Blake, visionary Master of
            Imagination.

                        BLAKE
            Imagination leads one to where the
            sun does not set. We come to teach
            you outside of time.

Written words and pictures from Blake's works flow from Blake to Robert. This figure disappears as another, taller one takes its place. Zarathustra holds an ancient lantern forward. A curious light shines forth from it.

                        ZARATHUSTRA
            Whooo ammm IIII?

                        ROBERT
            Frederick Nietzsche, philosopher
            and healer of Values. I am honored.

                    NIETZSCHE
          Poisonous flies in the marketplace
          know not Value. Solitude is holy
          and shares the present sacred
          moment with you.

Written words from this great teacher flow into Robert. This
figure disappears as another takes its place. A globe of the
Earth is spinning between its palms.

                    EINSTEIN
          Whooo ammm IIII?

                    ROBERT
          Genius. Tamer of the Universe.

                    EINSTEIN
          Whooo arrre youuu?

                    ROBERT
          A Seeker of Truth.

Symbols and formulae flow into Robert. This figure disappears
as another takes its place, its left hand is holding a paint
brush.

                    DA VINCI
          Whooo ammm IIII?

                    ROBERT
          Leonardo da Vinci. Magnificent
          Masterpiece of the Soul of Man.

                    DA VINCI
          The masterpiece is perfecting
          Intuitive Wisdom.

Magnificent art flows into Robert. This figure disappears as
another takes its place.

                    GOETHE
          Whooo ammm IIII?

                    ROBERT
          Johann Wolfgang von Goethe.
          Profound Revealer of Human
          Potential.

                    GOETHE
          Whooo arrre youuuu?

                    ROBERT
          I am nothing.

Goethe's written wisdom flows into Robert, book titles and all. This figure disappears as another takes its place.

          TWITCHELL
Whooo ammm IIII?

          ROBERT
Paul Twitchell. Cliff Hanger.
Master Revealer of the Light and
Sound.

          TWITCHELL
Dare to question cultural
conditioning. Open your symbols.

All of Paul's works flow into Robert. This figure disappears as another takes its place. In its right hand is a Vajra. In its left hand is a blue lotus.

          BUDDHA
Whooo ammm IIII?

          ROBERT
Shakyamuni Buddha. Bodhisattva on
High, in a World of Suffering.

Buddha points at Robert with the Vajra.

          BUDDHA
Whooo arrre Youuu?

This figure starts fading away as all the Sutras flow into Robert.

          BUDDHA (CONT'D)
Whooo arrre youuu?
   {Quieter}

          BUDDHA (CONT'D)
Whooo arrre youuu?

The thunderous peal has turned back into a waterfall, and then just a trickle, and it is out. Profound silence. Robert is sitting there all alone.

          ROBERT
Who am I?

HAWKWIND plays Looking In The Future:

"Lives of Great Men all remind us, we may make our lives sublime, and so departing, leave behind us, footprints in the sands of time.

"And with the writing, I will show you, looking in the days beyond recall, as I lecture with the Spirits on the other side, the other side. I'm living in the future, I'm looking at the past. I'm living in the future, I'm looking at the past."

INT. KATHY'S BATHROOM - 1976

Kathy is sitting lotus style on the counter top facing the mirror. Her fingers are sweeping through her hair in front of her face. She is searching for split ends and with each one she finds, she breaks the hair off between her fingernails and moves to the next one. Her expressions are ranging from DEEP in thought to no-thought contemplations.

Robert walks by the open door and catches her figure in the corner of his eye. He retraces a couple of steps to be back in the doorway.

                    ROBERT
        Hey! Are you okay?

Kathy nods her head.

                    ROBERT (CONT'D)
        You don't look okay.

                    KATHY
        I am fine.

Robert starts to move on but stops again.

                    ROBERT
        This isn't the first time I have
        seen you like this. What's wrong?

Kathy is afraid to cross some invisible barrier.

                    KATHY
        I just, I just don't know.

                    ROBERT
        You know I've told you, you can
        <u>always</u> come to me. Just be honest
        with me, that's all I ask.

Kathy nods.

                    ROBERT (CONT'D)
        Something is terribly wrong, isn't
        it?

Kathy moves to come down off the counter top and her ankle chain breaks and slides across the floor.

Robert looks at it, stunned.

> ROBERT (CONT'D)
> Our bond is broken... But why?

Kathy can see the truth of this as well, which gives her the courage to speak up with deathly seriousness.

> KATHY
> I will leave you soon.

> ROBERT
> Why?

> KATHY
> I can't live with you any longer. {DEEP breath} And I can't live without you.

Kathy moves toward the bedroom for the night. Stunned even further, Robert slowly walks into the living room and reaches for the mini-TV off knob just as the weatherman is talking.

> WEATHERMAN
> ...possibility of chinook winds coming over the range into the Denver/Boulder area tonight. It could gale up to 90 miles per hour.

Click.

Robert sits down lotus style in the middle of the livingroom floor. His suspicions were true. She is fascinated by another man. Hustler Jon. Con Man Extraordinaire.

Robert stares at the wall as it gets darker. He doesn't get up to turn on the light. Silence. His black kitten slinks over and nestles in his lap. He doesn't pet her for the first time ever. He is completely motionless. His heart is empty. Frozen. His mind is blank. "Gone, gone, gone to the Beyond."

QUEEN plays Who Wants To Live Forever:

"There's no time for us, there's no place for us. What is this thing that builds our dreams, yet slips away from us? Who wants to live forever? Who wants to live forever?

"There's no chance for us, it's all decided for us. This world has only one sweet moment set aside for us. Who wants to live forever? Who dares to love forever, when love must die!"

Yet, the kitten touches something hidden DEEP inside, reaching him much later, that tells him he is still somehow loved, no matter what happens in life.

An hour passes and the wind picks up and knocks at the window with a lonely wail. Robert continues to sit there into the wee hours of the morning, knowing that this is a huge shifting point of his life. He is beyond tears, beyond emotion. He doesn't care if the world is coming to an end. For him, it already has. There is no turning back.

The wind stops suddenly. We see a wisp of a red glow come out of the top of his head. Robert collapses onto his side and into a fitful sleep. His ankle chain falls off, broken. Jetsun Milarepa, look upon this poor, broken Soul with mercy.

HP LOVECRAFT II music plays the Blue Jack Of Diamonds:

"Once upon a time there was a King and a Queen, King and Queen of Hearts in their right. Then one day the King awoke and no one was there; She had stolen into the night.

"Can this be happening? Is there no answer here? It's not their love that had died, but no one was aware."

MONTAGE: SACRED CEREMONY EVENTS - 1984

Native American sacred ceremonies and dances are calling to Robert. He leaves Boulder and comes down into Southern Colorado.

HAWKWIND music is playing Black Elk Speaks:

"Grandfather, Great Mysterious One, you have been always, and before you, nothing has been. There is nothing to pray to but you. The Star Nations all over the Universe are yours, and yours are the grasses of the Earth. Day in, day out, you are the Light of All things."

Robert drives by a sign that says Welcome to Telluride. Robert is seen at a Native Faire. Fry bread is boiling in pots. Various people are making crafts and some small groups are moving slowly with the Tai Chi-like Tsalagi Dance of Life. He joins them to learn this one.

HAWKWIND continues: "Sweeten my heart and fill me with life. Give me the strength to understand, and the eyes to see. Help me! For without you, I am Nothing! Hetchetu Aloh!"

Robert drives by another sign saying Mount Hesperus. People are seen building Sound Chambers with Beautiful Painted Arrow. People are hoop dancing to big log drums. The Native visionary is leading the events. He bonds with Robert.

Robert sees a sign that reads Bodega Bay. We see a Medicine Wheel ceremony.

EXT. REDWOODS - GRAND-PA ROBERTS

DEEP in the Redwood Forest, we see a tall elderly Native American. He has a round belly, long gray beard, and gray hair down to below his shoulders. He's hugging a redwood tree. Robert is coming up a trail and spots him.

HAWKWIND song ends: "So, go on my friend! And sing with the Healing Spirit, with the magic of the Ground, with the magic of the Earth, and you will spring to life through the Power of the Words, through the magic of the Ground, through the magic of the Earth!"

Curious, Robert cuts off the trail and comes up to the man, inexplicably compelled to invade his personal space.

                    ROBERT
     I used to do that a bit when I was
     a young explorer of consciousness.

The Cherokee Elder turns toward Robert and looks right through him.

                  GRAND-PA ROBERTS
     What makes you think you're so old,
     young man?

                    ROBERT
     {Stunned} You look so familiar to
     me....

                  GRAND-PA ROBERTS
     You didn't answer my question.

Robert, master of bluntness himself, becomes uncomfortable with those blunt words. But, looking into the old man's eyes, he relaxes, just like with the Being in the barn decades ago.

                    ROBERT
     I've been hurt. Really hurt.

                  GRAND-PA ROBERTS
     I can see that!

Robert hesitates for a moment before going on.

                    ROBERT
     I need to... heal this pain inside
     me.

The wise man whispers to himself and looks around until he spots a huge redwood. Part of its center is gone and its insides are blackened by fire. He looks at Robert and points at the tree.

>   GRAND-PA ROBERTS
>   You need to go hug that tree. Be
>   One with that tree, and draw from
>   its Ancient Wisdom.

Robert walks over to the tree and sees its gutted interior. He shivers and then hugs the tree. After a bit, he relaxes and then walks back to the shaman.

>   GRAND-PA ROBERTS (CONT'D)
>   {With a knowing smile on his face}
>   Well?

>   ROBERT
>   I feel better now... but, I don't
>   even know why I hugged the tree or
>   even opened up like that to you in
>   the first place... except you look
>   so familiar to me. {Laughs} Almost
>   like a grand-father of mine.

>   GRAND-PA ROBERTS
>   {Chuckles} Well, they do call me
>   Grand-Pa Roberts.

>   ROBERT
>   Roberts? My name is Robert!

Grand-Pa sizes up the "young" man.

>   GRAND-PA ROBERTS
>   It is about time you found me,
>   Robert. I have been waiting for you
>   for some time now.

>   ROBERT
>   {Not surprised} You are a Shaman,
>   aren't you?

>   GRAND-PA ROBERTS
>   {Smiles knowingly} Some call me
>   that. Many call me Medicine Man.

>   ROBERT
>   How did you know I was looking for
>   a Shaman these last few months?

Grand-Pa launches into a well-known story of his.

                    GRAND-PA ROBERTS
          I am considered an old man at 94.
          But these trees are much older and
          wiser than I. Some trees have roots
          that reach far down into the Earth.
          Some trees have branches that reach
          far up into the Sky. Their reach is
          much greater than mine. Hugging the
          right tree not only bring healing
          but also wisdom in new visions.

Grand-Pa sizes him up again and shifts to a more personal
tone, reserved for a very few.

                    GRAND-PA ROBERTS (CONT'D)
          I remember through these trees that
          three of us came down to Earth in
          1890 in order to accomplish
          specific tasks during the time of
          the Fifth Cleansing. One brother is
          in Tibet, the other brother is in
          Europe. I have spoken with them.
          They recollect this with me.

Robert is floored with what he has just heard! He thought no
one else had an unbelievably strange memory like this!

                    ROBERT
          Wow! Grand-Pa! I remember nine of
          us coming down in 1950! Only four
          of us have survived thus far!

Grand-Pa somehow already knows this about him.

                    GRAND-PA ROBERTS
          You, Robert, are the second wave of
          our task and I know you are feeling
          the truth of these words as I
          speak. We have known each other
          before this measured time. I
          recognize you, too. You are a
          kindred Soul. You are a rainbow
          person. I can see it in your eyes.
          You transcend and embrace All
          Tribes. Are you prepared for the
          next leg of your life's journey?

There was no doubt, no hesitation, just a firm...

                    ROBERT
          Yes!

Robert felt like he embraced All Tribes... but little did he
know at the time to what extent. How amazingly prophetic!

Decades away from true fulfilment! These long forgotten words of Grand-Pa will reach far into the future!

EXT. GRAND-PA'S POD HOUSE - 1985

We see people standing in front of Grand-Pa's pod house. One person walks in. We see Grand-Pa and the person talking. Grand-Pa places a crystal gently into the person's hand.

EXT. GRAND-PA'S LAND

We see Robert carving out the hard pack dirt of the hillside into more defined steps for the convenience of Grand-Pa and the others who come down from the road, walking the 410 foot slant to his Pod house.

EXT. GRAND-PA'S POD HOUSE

We see Grand-Pa come out with someone else. Grand-Pa points to a tree and the person walks over to the tree to hug it as Grand-Pa reenters the pod house. Another person walks in from the queue. We see them exchange crystals and talk.

EXT. GRAND-PA'S LAND

We see Robert collecting wood. A few sentinel bees come out of the ground and swarm Robert. The pack responds in kind. Robert drops the wood and starts hollering as he runs.

EXT. GRAND-PA'S POD HOUSE

Grand-Pa comes bursting out the door.

                    GRAND-PA ROBERTS
Cougar!

We see the men run toward each other. Grand-Pa spies the bees and starts laughing. Strangely enough, the bees seem to respond to that laugh and spontaneously return back to the ground. Robert is very animated, flapping his jacket and scratching his beard... which makes Grand-Pa laugh even harder. Finally he reaches over and plucks a bee from Robert's beard and releases it to the air.

                    GRAND-PA ROBERTS (CONT'D)
There we go. Off with you! Oops, there's another one. Allow me!

ROBERT
{Gasping} That's incredible! They're all gone! They know you!

GRAND-PA ROBERTS
Those little brothers know I wouldn't hurt them. {Winks at him} It's all about who you know. {Laughs and turns more serious} It's all really about intentions.

ROBERT
There was a black swarm around me, and no where to hide!

GRAND-PA ROBERTS
So where do you go when you can't hide?

ROBERT
What could I do? I was surprised and terrified... and just reacted naturally.

GRAND-PA ROBERTS
Reacting naturally can get you in trouble. Sometimes you need to override your survival instinct.

ROBERT
How do I do that?

GRAND-PA ROBERTS
Right Intentions and will power. It's easy once you have the Right Intentions.

ROBERT
{Calming down} What do you mean by "Right Intentions"?

GRAND-PA ROBERTS
Become the bee. Love it, not fear it. Become One with the bee.

ROBERT
So are there spiritual instincts that go beyond the human?

                    GRAND-PA ROBERTS
          {Grins} You got it! The more you
          focus on having the Right
          Intentions, the more they will just
          be there by instinct when you need
          them most.

EXT. OVERHEAD SHOT TO FOREST BELOW

We see a twelve foot diameter Medicine Wheel made of rocks
interspersed with crystals and the like. Grand-Pa is sitting
inside the North end of the Wheel facing the center with a
drum. He is on a bearskin rug. Robert is sitting cross-legged
in the South facing the center. We hear an eagle sounding in
the distance. As Grand-Pa drums, the camera slowly zooms to
Grand-Pa from Robert's perspective. The drumming stops.

                    GRAND-PA ROBERTS
          I can sense you work mainly with
          four Sweet Medicine animals. I will
          now connect you to each of their
          Spirit forms so you may more fully
          integrate with them.

Grand-Pa drums and chants rhythmically.

                    GRAND-PA ROBERTS (CONT'D)
          Tiv-da-tsi... Cougar...
          Asqua-nigo-hisdi... Surprise...
          We-hali... Eagle...
          Dili-gota-nuhi-ada-nudo...
          Connection to Spirit...
          I'na-du... Snake...
          Di-ne-tlana... Creation...
          Yona... Bear
          Asgi-tsga... Dreamer.

INT. CAMERA ZOOMS INTO ROBERT'S MIND

We see each of these Sweet Medicine animals individually in
their own habitats as Grand-Pa calls them out. Robert is now
honored and called by his main Medicine name, Cougar... It
becomes a legal middle name change. More sacred is Grand-Pa
receiving words in Visioning through the Great Spirit
Medicine, descending for Robert as Golden Sky Cougar.

MONTAGE: MEDICINE WHEEL TRANSFORMATION - 1987

Camera zooms back out from Cougar's head into the sky, this
time higher. The drumming continues but is replaced with a
DEEPER, more powerful group drum.

As the camera zooms back down, instead of a rock Medicine Wheel, we see a human Medicine Wheel moving and dancing.

Closer, we see an outer circle of about ten people, mostly men moving clockwise. We see an inner circle of about seven people, mostly women, moving counterclockwise.

The camera pans outside the circle to a small group of four people with large sticks beating in unison on a large Grandfather Drum. We see Grand-Pa is one of those four.

We scan back to the dance circle and see Cougar in the outer circle dancing with the movements of his Sweet Medicine animals, moving fluidly from one form to another. There are no voices, only DEEP drumming. Some of the dancers are changing places from one circle to the next.

The drumming stops abruptly. All join hands into a larger circle. Grand-Pa breaks hands with his Co-Weaver and heads clockwise into the center space until all are close together. They breathe together and contemplate intentions danced out.

The Co-Weaver, Sedonia, gently guides the circle out counterclockwise until they are back out into the larger circle again.

      GRAND-PA AND SEDONIA
 Ah-ho!

Everyone squeezes hands and lets go. Conversations start in little groups. Cougar walks out into the woods with Sedonia.

      SEDONIA
   It has been a real pleasure having
   you in our dance the last couple of
    years.

      COUGAR
   Thank-you, Sedonia. This dance
   means a lot to me. Each month the
   dance seems totally different than
   the last. It always surprises me. I
   grow in different ways each time.

      SEDONIA
   Yes. It has that effect on most of
   us.

      COUGAR
   And to think at my first dance you
   and the others had to convince me
   to join in and when I finally did,
   I didn't stop dancing for hours
   until the end. No breaks.

SEDONIA
That was so funny how that went for you. My heart is gladdened, Cougar!

COUGAR
Both The Dance and Grand-Pa himself seem to be powerful healers for many people who come here.

SEDONIA
He is such a heart-filled Medicine Man, isn't he?

COUGAR
I would have never expected a Cherokee Elder to nest in California.

SEDONIA
He lives in the moment.

COUGAR
He is at home anywhere! Sometimes you can't even get him out of the grocery store. He will stand there and talk to everyone... even any stranger he meets!

SEDONIA
That's right! That definitely taught me patience and to be more observant of others.

COUGAR
I still hear an occasional story from people that halfway down the four hundred foot step trail, Seekers feel his love hugging them like a warm blanket. I myself feel his love-aura to be that huge. It's like no one else's I have ever felt!

The couple walk a little further in silence and then...

SEDONIA
I certainly appreciate you house sitting for me this week. I am off to facilitate a group healing ceremony in the desert.

COUGAR
I am glad to do it and am glad for you. Explore... and Enjoy yourself.

SEDONIA
Thank you, Cougar. I will see you when I get back.

They part with a hug and Sedonia leaves Cougar at her door...

SEDONIA (CONT'D)
{With a backward glance, yelling}
And why the heck you haven't fallen for any of those beautiful women who come to the dance beats the heck out of me!

COUGAR
{Shouting} The Sacred Dance IS My Sacred Woman!

SEDONIA
{Mumbling} For now.

INT. SEDONIA'S CABIN - ONE DAY LATER

We hear a knock on the door. Cougar gets up from a meditation to answer it. A lovely woman with long hair is standing there holding a towel in her hand.

AMANDA
Sedonia? Is she here?

COUGAR
She has gone away for a week or so.

AMANDA
Oh, I didn't know! She must have gotten over her cold. I am Amanda, a friend of hers. We hold monthly healing ceremonies here for women. They are pretty powerful. Female energy, you know. May I come in for a moment?

Cougar pushes the door open further and Amanda saunters in.

AMANDA (CONT'D)
You must be Cougar!

COUGAR
I am.

AMANDA
I have heard a lot about you.

>COUGAR
>I hope it has only been good.

>AMANDA
>Certainly has. Hey, you don't mind if I take a bath here? Sedonia lets me do that whenever I have trouble with my hot water.

Cougar is speechless but gracefully holds his hand out to the bath. She goes in and leaves the door ajar, hoping he cannot resist watching her.

Amanda is singing sweetly while Cougar continues to meditate lotus style with his back to her door.

Amanda then talks some but Cougar is not listening or responding. A gray form swirls up near the ceiling behind him for a little while and disappears. Amanda finishes her bath and comes out, only in her towel.

>AMANDA (CONT'D)
>Thank-you so much, Cougar, for letting me bathe. Don't mind me, I am just borrowing some clean clothes from Sedonia.

Amanda changes right behind him but he doesn't turn around until she is finished.

>AMANDA (CONT'D)
>Sedonia tells me you travel out of body sometimes.

>COUGAR
>Yes.

>AMANDA
>Sedonia doesn't care to try that sort of thing but I have travelled out of body a bit myself and enjoy it.

>COUGAR
>Really? I don't hear many people tell me that! And those that do, usually fear it.

>AMANDA
>I also enjoy Tantric sex.

>COUGAR
>You do?

                    AMANDA
          Yes, I am <u>very</u> experienced with
          Tantric sex and travelling out of
          body. I've done both with several
          men. It's exciting!

Cougar rolls his eyes, disappointed, once again.

                    COUGAR
          It is a very sacred thing to do.

Cougar stands up. Amanda approaches him and wraps her arms around him.

                    AMANDA
          I am available for now.

Cougar's body does not respond to her touch, except to place his hands absently on her hips.

                    COUGAR
          Sorry, not today. I am feeling a
          bit moody.

The couple break contact and Amanda heads for the door. She remains upbeat.

                    AMANDA
          Come up to my place sometime. I
          will show you some beautiful
          crystals I have gathered.

Amanda spies a black, spiky rock around three inches in diameter and touches it.

                    AMANDA (CONT'D)
          Oh, Sedonia has forgotten to mail
          this back to Hawaii. She has been
          meaning to. It's bad luck to take
          volcanic rock. Good intentions,
          though. She thought it would aid
          our female ceremonies.

She points a finger at him.

                    AMANDA (CONT'D)
          Don't forget to look me up.

Cougar nods, but with slightly disapproving eyes and goes back to his meditation position.

DREAMSCAPE THAT NIGHT

Disturbed by the earlier sexual enticement, Cougar has a dream of Kathy. He is seen placing their ankle chains on in their spontaneous ceremony of the past. A loving moment.

FLEETWOOD MAC plays Never Break The Chain: "Listen to the wind blow, watch the sunrise. Run in the shadows."

Cougar sees how Spirit severed the chain from her ankle as she slid off the counter top... and then not much later, from his own. A great mystery, indeed! Spirit knew how she fell into another's arms, breaking their bond made in Heaven.

FLEETWOOD MAC: "Damn your love, damn your lies! I can still hear you saying, you would never break the chain."

Cougar sees Kathy by the Great Ocean once again. The waves are sparkling those rainbow colors of the past.

FLEETWOOD MAC: "And if you don't love me now, you will never love me again, I can still hear you saying, you would never break the chain."

They hug with great tears in their eyes. She lets go of him, turns away and slowly walks into the Ocean. The water moves up to her neck. Not looking back, she slips into THE DEEP... forever?

FLEETWOOD MAC: "Chain, keep us together! Running in the shadow. Chain keep us together, run in the shadow."

Cougar wakes up and quickly sits up. Loud breathy whisper...

     COUGAR
 Wowww! It has been twelve years
 since I've seen her! Wowww!

MONTAGE: SEDONIA'S HOUSE

The next day we see Cougar walking on Sedonia's land enjoying the privacy of a few acres. Approaching her cabin, he spies the bushes overgrown up to the cabin walls. Finding clippers in the open slant space under the cabin, Cougar trims away.

Cougar finds a shovel. He digs out some better dirt steps leading down to her front door, fortunately less than ten.

We see Cougar trimming more bushes. Cougar scratches his arms and coughs. He doesn't realize he has been in Poison Oak.

Cougar is laying on the back deck, looking up at the cloudless sky. Tiny birds traverse far up in the sky.

Millions of little dots of light begin specking the sky, dancing. The magic of it is transporting.

Cougar goes into the cabin and meditates cross-legged. He starts scratching his arms. He goes over to the sink and washes his hands and arms. He sits to meditate. He scratches his arms and coughs.

Dusk is settling in. A darker gray swirl appears behind him, larger and more menacing. Cougar does not see the swirl but feels it. This is more than female ceremony magic residue.

Cougar panics and jumps up and runs out the door, up the dirt stairs and through the woods. An owl hoots. The menacing cloud follows him, along with the owl.

EXT. TO INT. GRAND-PA'S POD HOUSE

Just as total darkness descends, Cougar knocks on the door, panting. Grand-Pa bids him enter. Cougar runs into the middle of the room. Grand-Pa stands up.

> GRAND-PA ROBERTS
> Something wrong, son?

> COUGAR
> Grand-Pa! Something is seriously wrong!

> GRAND-PA ROBERTS
> What is troubling you so? I haven't seen you like this.

> COUGAR
> It is like LSD or something! The trees came alive on the way over here! It felt like good and evil were clashing out there in the woods. An owl followed me all the way!

> GRAND-PA ROBERTS
> Slow down son, you aren't making any sense!

Cougar takes a couple of DEEP breaths. Grand-Pa puts a hand to Cougar's forehead.

> GRAND-PA ROBERTS (CONT'D)
> Feels like you got yourself quite a fever!

COUGAR
I have been feeling odd the last few days between the cold I caught and the Poison Oak. But now I feel like I'm being led to the edge of a precipice.

GRAND-PA ROBERTS
What do you mean?

COUGAR
Well, at first I thought there was a ghost in Sedonia's house. I have exorcised ghosts from houses before, so I thought that was all I'd have to do at Sedonia's. I connected with it for a brief time and thought I sent it on its merry way. A surge of light flooded the house. Everything got brighter and I knew it was gone... but it fooled me and snuck back in later. It was as if it was hiding itself from me on purpose.

GRAND-PA ROBERTS
That's odd.

COUGAR
Yes, and then with this fever, I have been getting very hot and the next moment, I am freezing. My mind feels like it split in two, between logic and emotions. I meditate like I am reaching a portal between life and death. Just one heartbeat away!

All of a sudden the owl hoots again close by. Grand-Pa's eyes grow very large as he looks directly into Cougar's Soul. All is quiet for a long moment.

GRAND-PA ROBERTS
Remember my teaching of the Owl?

Cougar nods his head in agreement.

GRAND-PA ROBERTS (CONT'D)
Some tribes welcome the owl as a messenger of Life and some tribes fear it as the messenger of Death. The owl is not evil in itself.

COUGAR
Yes? Grand-Pa?

> GRAND-PA ROBERTS
> Death has come for you! Sedonia should have sent back that black rock from Hawaii. I will deal with that tomorrow. But for now...

> COUGAR
> What do you mean Death has come for me?

> GRAND-PA ROBERTS
> I see that you are about to go to a place where no one returns. The few who somehow survive, come back insane!

Cougar clutches his heart in confusion. Grand-Pa grabs Cougar by the shoulders to support him from falling.

> COUGAR
> Grand-Pa, can you help me?

> GRAND-PA ROBERTS
> We must get you to the Medicine Wheel! Now!... No! I will stay here and seal the path with sacred salts. This is a fey initiation. You must listen to me. Don't worry about the Owl. Get down the trail to the Medicine Wheel and stay there as long as it takes. You will know when it is okay to come back. I will protect you. Wrap my love around you like a blanket.

Cougar turns to go. At the door, he turns back to Grand-Pa.

> COUGAR
> But Grand-Pa, I am weak. What do I do if I can no longer feel love?

> GRAND-PA ROBERTS
> Then open a door _to_ love. Always open the door to love. Go now. I know you can do it. I will drum for you here and hold the space clear.

EXT. MEDICINE WHEEL - MOONLIT NIGHT

Cougar goes to the edge of the Medicine Wheel in the gray dark of the night with no flashlight. Moon glow is enough. The owl hoots in the distance. It has not followed him here. Grand-Pa Roberts' drumming can be heard in the distance.

HAWKWIND short song, Joker At The Gate begins:

"People function, dreaming their dreams. People function, scheming their schemes. People function, trusting to Fate, looking for the Joker but it's too late."

Cougar steps into the center of the Medicine Wheel and sits down facing South, the direction of the Pod house where he came from.

HAWKWIND Joker: "Is there still a moment somewhere, that will surprise us with its tricks?"

The trees begin to move menacingly around him. Cougar swoons and slumps forward, passing out.

HAWKWIND ends: "I am the Holder of Seven dreams, faceless possessor of all life's schemes. Through me you can laugh in the face of Fate. I am the Joker at your Gate!"

INT. PIT OF DARKNESS

Cougar wakes up dead! He sees himself balancing on a 2 foot wide bridge of steel that spans a distance of at least fifty yards on both ends into the darkness. The bridge has a slight arc. There is no support below the bridge.

He then sees he is suspended in a huge Pit that narrows toward the top about the size of the 12 foot Medicine Wheel. He can see light at the top where the world he has come from lies out of reach. There is an undefined sense of Dread in this Pit. Cougar yearns for the live world above. He watches as the opening at the top of the Pit narrows down to nothing. The light above is gone.

Cougar is stripped naked in an instant. He is also cold as Hell, quite literally. Love has abandoned him.

    COUGAR
 {Whispers} I've lost my
 Immortality. How can this be?

INT. DARK THRONE ROOM

Out of the darkness, Cougar, looking downward, can see two glistening globs of Blackness that appear to be alive. The growing light shows this to be the Throne Room of Hell. Telepathically, they speak.

    DARK GREAT GRAND-MOTHER & FATHER
 Welcome home, our Son.

COUGAR
I am not your son.

DARK GREAT GRAND-MOTHER & FATHER
Hah hah hah. You think not? You are our kindred, our spawn. You are our chosen one.

COUGAR
I don't know you.

DARK GREAT GRAND-MOTHER & FATHER
We are your Ancestors. You belong to us. You cannot deny us.

Cougar can feel invisible tentacles reach up to him and wrap around the very cells of his Soul. Cougar looks up to Heaven but no light comes. He calls out but the top is sealed shut.

COUGAR
God. Buddha. Jesus! Anyone! Muhammad. Michael. Rafael. Save me from this mess! Let me know you are real! I don't belong here!

DARK GREAT GRAND-MOTHER
They do not hear you. You belong to us. You are our progeny. I am Lilith, your Dark Great Grandmother.

DARK GREAT GRAND-FATHER
Don't you remember us? I am your Dark Great Grandfather, Sama-El.

COUGAR
No! Get out of my head!

SAMA-EL
You have passed the boundary of lawful Knowledge by coming here. We were here long before the beginning of time. There are no other Gods before us. We will show you who you really are, Cougar.

EXT. CREATION

The Dark Couple show Cougar their version of Creation. Half truth and half lie makes it very convincing. The Big Bang. Stars flying out into space. Eventually cooling. Now, spiny spores are seen floating through space and into the atmosphere of the Earth.

> SAMA-EL
> Life migrated to Earth, hungry to eat. We were cunning to adapt to any circumstance and develop into everything, hungry to prey and to be preyed upon. We all rely on Death in order to Live. We all kill in order to live and evolve. No one escapes this killing fate!

Scenes are given to Cougar to show life growing and devouring itself and consuming the planet. It is like a glorified cancer mutating while eating everything in its path.

> COUGAR
> Thank you for your story, but no thanks! I would like to leave now.

> SAMA-EL
> You can never leave. This is Life. The seeds of the Ancestor live in the Son. Embrace us! We need you! Join us. You have risen above the turbulent Herd of Men... Those wretched Mundanes! Ostriches, All! You may have any of the Daughters of the Earth you so desire.

INT. DARK HALL OF FEASTING

The Creation story of the world is gone and Cougar now finds himself in a Hallway of Feasting. There are Seven Great Conquerors of the Earth that parade by him one at a time. As History is shown him, some are seen fighting on horseback, some are seen feasting with women. Slaves of all colors are serving them in fear. All the Proud are laughing and shouting war cries. They all beckon Cougar to join them now.

Cougar is torn between heightened lust by resisting and a sickening gut by joining. Cougar lurches forward and backward and ends up staying his ground, barefoot and naked on the cold steel arc of the narrow bridge.

INT. DARK THRONE ROOM

> LILITH AND SAMA-EL
> Whatever you want, it is yours-
> Money, Fame, Power, Women, Men.
> Anything! Name it!

Lilith and Sama-El point at Cougar. A mirror appears before him. His eyes start to glow.

> SAMA-EL
> See, you have The Power! You know it's real. You have used it on Earth before, use it again!

> COUGAR
> But there is no way I can get away with this kind of Power. People will fear me. People will stop me.

> SAMA-EL
> They will never suspect. There is a natural veil that hides Power from mortal eyes, especially Mundanes!

Cougar is shown a psychic mist that will cover the power in his eyes.

> SAMA-EL (CONT'D)
> See how easy it is? Just a mere thought, a mere glance at them and they will do your bidding unaware! You are unstoppable. You are ripe for great Conquest and great Glory! Come back to us! You are family!

All of the Conquerors shout for Cougar in the background. This is too much for Cougar. No one came to save him and he must make a decision now. It has gone on too long.

> COUGAR
> With due respect. Thank you for your offer, but no thanks.

> LILITH AND SAMA-EL
> Are you sure? What do you want?

> COUGAR
> I want to leave now.

> LILITH AND SAMA-EL
> What do you want? Anything, everything is yours for the taking.

> COUGAR
> Thanks, but I want to leave now.

The Dark Couple have instantly turned angry and threatening.

> SAMA-EL
> You can never leave us! The only way to leave us is to die! Do you want to live or to die?

                    COUGAR
          I want to live.

                    SAMA-EL
          Join us Eternally or die, Mortal!
          What is your choice?

Cougar knows this is the end and fights against his survival instinct, as Grand-Pa has shown him.

                    COUGAR
          There is no choice. I will <u>not</u> join
           you!

                    LILITH AND SAMA-EL
          How dare you! Then die, Mortal! You
          will be extinguished Forever! Do
          you not understand?

Cougar sees no choice but to surrender to his Fate.

                    COUGAR
          All too well. I would rather not
          exist than exist with you in pain
          forever.

Lilith and Sama-El both point their fingers at Cougar and a great light comes forth from both the Dark Couple's heads and attacks Cougar's head. All goes black for a long moment.

EXT. MEDICINE WHEEL - DAWN COMES

We see Cougar slumped over on his side, motionless. A couple of bees are heard coming near his head and flying off. This wakes Cougar. He looks around and sits up. He feels his body and realizing he is alive, he jumps up and moves out of the Medicine Wheel as fast as he can.

The two bees come back and face off with his eyes less than two feet away. This causes him to stop. He moves to get around them and yet they stay on point, no matter what his antics are to prove this isn't really happening on purpose.

Cougar finally gets it. He backs up into the Medicine Circle to give thanks to it for the protection it gave and to honor the Four basic Directions. He is too much in shock of his fresh experience with the struggle of the Above and the Below, in terms of Good and Evil, to do the Six Directions.

The bees leave him as quickly as they came. Cougar does not hesitate to flee himself!

EXT. GRAND-PA'S POD HOUSE

Grand-Pa is hugging Cougar at his doorway. Cougar's arms are down at his side. He is weary. Grand-Pa pushes away to arm's length while holding Cougar's shoulders.

> GRAND-PA ROBERTS
> Blessings Be to The Great Spirit! You have come back to me!

> COUGAR
> Am I not dead?

> GRAND-PA ROBERTS
> You are fine, Cougar. You eyes are a little wild, but clear.

> COUGAR
> I have come from the place of No Love. Absolutely none. In that Dark Pit, love simply does not exist. Power, power is everything.

> GRAND-PA ROBERTS
> Would you like to sit on it and have some tea?

> COUGAR
> I need time to process this stuff. I need to get away from here.

Grand-Pa shakes Cougar.

> GRAND-PA ROBERTS
> Come back in three days.

They both hug.

EXT. GRAND-PA'S PORCH - THREE DAYS LATER

Grand-Pa and Cougar are sitting in chairs on the wrap around porch. They are soaking in the sun and the trees and life all around them. The green is leaning in as delightful cover.

> GRAND-PA ROBERTS
> Cougar, have you heard of the Goddess Inanna?

> COUGAR
> Can't say I have.

> GRAND-PA ROBERTS
> You have heard of Ishtar, yes?

COUGAR
Wasn't she the Goddess of Love or fertility or something?

GRAND-PA ROBERTS
There you go, son. Inanna was the prototype of Ishtar some seven thousand years ago, or more.

Cougar savors the name.

COUGAR
Inanna...

GRAND-PA ROBERTS
I seem to remember a story about Inanna taking a Journey to Hell herself. The first of the Tragic Journeys to Hell in recorded history, no less!

COUGAR
Oh?

GRAND-PA ROBERTS
The things you say about your experiences reminds me of her story. Inanna went to Hell grasping a Golden Ring in her hand much like in your motorcycle crash thirteen years ago.

COUGAR
Really!!

GRAND-PA ROBERTS
And now <u>this</u> experience of yours. She was an Immortal stripped naked in Hell. The Anunnaki gazed upon her with the eyes of the accursed. The Immortal Inanna was sickened to death and hung on a steel pike, not too far off from being suspended on your narrow steel bridge.

COUGAR
But I miraculously survived!

GRAND-PA ROBERTS
So did she! Father Enki, one of the Anunnaki, the most compassionate of the Gods, created two bees to fly the gates of Hell and rescue her!

COUGAR
Two bees! I was greeted by two bees when I found myself on top the Pit!

GRAND-PA ROBERTS
Yes, indeed!

COUGAR
Anunnaki? Who are these Anunnaki?

GRAND-PA ROBERTS
They were the Seven Judges of Hell.

COUGAR
Kind of like the Seven Conquerors I saw in Hell who were given power on Earth and Hell by the Dark Couple.

GRAND-PA ROBERTS
Legend has it that the Seven Judges of Hell were sometimes shown as the Seven Gods of Heaven as well.

COUGAR
You mean like the Seven Beings of Light I met in Heaven?

Grand-Pa nods.

GRAND-PA ROBERTS
Cougar, you are on a Journey of Epic proportions! You have tapped into the Universal Myth and proved it's a Reality and not just a Myth! It is a Spiritual Journey for All of us on Earth. How wonderful!

COUGAR
I don't feel so wonderful. I failed in my task. I did not defeat Darkness.

GRAND-PA ROBERTS
Cougar, you did not fail! You weren't there to <u>defeat</u> Darkness! You were tested and shown that you cannot be <u>compromised by</u> Darkness! That is no small deed! Look around you and tell me how many people are out there that you look up to, who have <u>not</u> been compromised at some point?

Cougar thinks for a long moment.

                    COUGAR
          Only you, Grand-pa. Only you.
          Everyone else has let me down.

Cougar breathes out a long sigh.

                    COUGAR (CONT'D)
          You seek neither fame nor fortune.
          You give freely to all who seek you
          out. I love you, Grand-Pa!

                    GRAND-PA ROBERTS
          You are like a son to me. A dear
          son. A kindred Soul.

They both get up for a big bear hug.

                    GRAND-PA ROBERTS (CONT'D)
          Now get down into town and get us
          some supplies.

                    COUGAR
          Ugh, Grand-Pa... I feel like hiding
          out forever.

Grand-Pa gives him a quizzical look.

                    COUGAR (CONT'D)
          I don't feel up to dealing with
          people quite yet.

                    GRAND-PA ROBERTS
          Go on now... It will do you some
          good to be with people... you'll
          see...

EXT. FORESTVILLE DRIVE

Cougar has three seconds per person to look into their eyes as they drive by in opposite directions. He gets a visual image of each person's burden as they drive by. Some are fresh family problems. Some are old wounds from childhood. Cougar is overwhelmed by the pain he feels and tries not to look any longer.

Cougar stops in Forestville and walks the last two blocks to the grocery store, trying as best he can to not look into people's eyes. Cougar senses someone in front of him who feels threatening. Someone is up to no good.

                    COUGAR
          {Thinks} I don't like you. Move off
          the side walk, guy.

This guy, twenty feet in front of him, practically jumps off
the sidewalk and into moving traffic. A car screeches its
tires and honks its horn. The man is almost hit.

                    COUGAR (CONT'D)
          {Thinks} Focus, Cougar. Focus on
          the task at hand. Do not wander...
          even for an instant.

Cougar successfully enters the store, avoiding eye contact
with everyone. He collects a hand basket and a few items off
the shelves. And then it happens! Cougar is near the back of
an aisle and his eye catches the figure of a woman waiting in
the check out lane. She has long hair, hair as black as the
Pit! It is draped ravenously over a red, one piece dress. The
dress tightly hugs her body and snakes only six inches or so
down her shapely thighs.

                    COUGAR (CONT'D)
          {Thinks} Wow!

Immediately, the Lady in Red responds to that thought. She
turns around and looks directly into his eyes.

                    COUGAR (CONT'D)
          {Thinks} She is beautiful! With
          just a casual thought, I... I could
          beckon her to me.

The Lady in Red breaks away from her female friend in line
and walks toward Cougar.

                    COUGAR (CONT'D)
          {Thinks} This is not happening. I
          will prove it's not. {And with a
          commanding thought} I want to be
          with you. I want to see what you
          look like naked. Don't hold back!

The closer she comes to him, the more beautiful she looks.
She starts pulling slowly at her shoulder straps. They drape
down across her tender yet firm biceps. Her rich tan makes
the red dress and black hair even more vibrant. She is still
looking directly into his eyes.

Twenty feet away from him, she looks like she is now walking
in slow motion. Cougar's jaw drops as he sees her dress is
slowly slithering down her tanned breasts with every step she
takes. She is now twelve feet away and still fastened on him.

                    COUGAR (CONT'D)
          {Thinks} I would sell my Soul for
          one week with you... my Soul...

With that thought, Cougar recovers his senses.

                    COUGAR (CONT'D)
          {Thinks} What have I done? Devil
          with the red dress, red dress on...

Cougar smiles at this song in his head and pretending to ignore her, turns toward a shelf. He removes any old can from the shelf and puts it in the basket. She stops at five feet.

The spell is broken! The Lady in Red looks around, dazed and embarrassed. She wriggles her hips and throws her straps up quickly and turns back to her friend.

In line, they exchange short sentences quickly and both look back at Cougar several times. Their expressions turn to fear. They cannot get out of the store too soon.

Cougar hears an echo of the Dark Couple.

                    LILITH AND SAMA-EL
          All this can be yours, if you give
          us your Soul. Do our bidding and we
          will fulfill all your needs. You
          are family! Return to us! Cougar!

EXT. GRAND-PA'S PORCH

                    GRAND-PA ROBERTS
          So, you are causing a bit of a stir
          in town, are ya?

                    COUGAR
          And I don't know what to do about
          it, Grand-Pa. It's like Darkness is
          clinging to me and I can't shake it
          off. They have followed me from the
          Pit. They won't give up. They still
          want me.

Grand-Pa sees Cougar's fear and puts his hand on Cougar's arm.

                    GRAND-PA ROBERTS
          Remember, Cougar, they know you are
          willing to give up your Mortal life
          to not fall into their dark
          schemes.
                         (MORE)

GRAND-PA ROBERTS (CONT'D)
They know you will go as far as giving up your Immortal Soul to not be part of them. How can they touch you now?

COUGAR
This dark energy is too much for me. I have to remember to watch my thoughts with every waking moment and even when I sleep! I look at someone and they will turn around to look at me. I can think someone to me. I can think someone away from me. Why did I end up in The Pit? Why is Darkness in the world? Why do they have it out for me?

GRAND-PA ROBERTS
{Says with some sadness} It is time for you to journey to Mount Shasta.

COUGAR
Mount Shasta? Why there, Grand-Pa?

GRAND-PA ROBERTS
If any place is going to clear your head and purify your heart, it's going to be the Sacred Mount Shasta... Go there, Cougar... Who knows, it may even break the other curse... like with Inanna!

Grand-Pa has a very troubled look on his brow.

COUGAR
What curse? I thought she died, and was revived, to live Immortal, once again?

GRAND-PA ROBERTS
She was, but there was one condition on her return to life.

Cougar stares intensely at Grand-Pa for his coming words.

GRAND-PA ROBERTS (CONT'D)
She also came back with Daemons clinging to her ankles.

Cougar's eyes grow wider.

GRAND-PA ROBERTS (CONT'D)
Unbeknownst to her, someone else had to take her place in Hell.

                    GRAND-PA ROBERTS (CONT'D)
          Against her will, it was Dumuzi,
          her beloved husband. Who knows if
          this really has to be the way of
          it? Who knows? For now, let us get
          you ready for Mount Shasta.

EXT. MOUNT SHASTA - SUMMIT

We see Cougar on the Summit facing South. A bota bag of water is strapped across his shoulder. That's it. No equipment, no special snow boots. A rainbow bubble aura is seen arcing with the horizon. The eagle's view is breathtaking.

Cougar slowly brings his arms out and up to the heart level. His hands are cupped toward each other. He is standing in a Kung Fu Healing stance for the Earth and for himself.

Cougar's aura is a golden hue from the light play. As soon as his hands reach a couple of inches from each other, a purple plume of light streams straight up from the Summit, through Cougar, into the sky. We hear a female voice in the distance softly calling. Shastina and/or Goddess Inanna?

                    SHASTINA
          Rroberrt...
          {Five to seven seconds later}
          Rroberrrtt Cougarrr.

                    COUGAR
          {Shouts} I am free! I am free!
          Magnificent! Thank-you, Great
          Spirit!

Cougar breaks his stance and starts leaping down The Mountain, full of life.

EXT. PANTHER CAMPGROUND - PRIMITIVE SITE

Altitude: 7,600 feet. Cougar is coming from the sacred spring with two fresh gallons of water, one in each hand. He almost reaches his campsite when he is met by two hippie clothed guys from Forestville.

                    WHITE FEATHER
          Cougar! What a place!

                    COUGAR
          White Feather! Wolf! How are you
          guys?

They do some hand shake dancing and then embrace.

COUGAR (CONT'D)
What brings you two up the Sacred Mountain?

WHITE FEATHER
We heard you were camped at Panther, so we came up.

COUGAR
Pull up a log and stay awhile.

WHITE FEATHER
We are just passing through but had to bring you the news.

COUGAR
What news is that?

WHITE FEATHER
It's Grand-Pa... he passed on three days ago.

COUGAR
Grand-Pa? No way! What happened?

WHITE FEATHER
His heart gave out... At least someone was with him when he passed and she said she witnessed a true Saint leave this world... and so peacefully happy.

COUGAR
{Stunned} Wow... I am glad someone was with him at the end.

WHITE FEATHER
What's more is, just the day before he died, he said he had seen a cougar go into his Medicine Circle and rest awhile. What made this noteworthy was that this was the first time he had seen a cougar come close to the Medicine Wheel, let alone enter it. He saw it as a sign that you were finished here and would return soon.

EXT. PANTHER MEADOW

Cougar walks to the center of the meadow and looks around to make sure that he is alone and starts shouting to the sky with his arms in the air.

                    COUGAR
          Grand-Pa!...
          Grand-Pa!...
          Why did you leave us now!...
          Now, of all times!...
          NO!...
          NO!...
          Grand-Pa!...
          NO!...
          It's not fair!...
          I am ready to see you again!...
          And now you are gone!...
          No!...
          Grand-Pa!...
          Why!...
          Why!...
          Why!...

Cougar collapses to his knees but finds he cannot cry. Smoothly, he moves into a lotus position and puts his hands on his knees, palms down. A butterfly lands on his arm. Cougar's gaze is steadfast in front, facing the Summit.

The sun begins to slide across the sky...Cougar stays motionless. One hour. Two hours. Butterflies are beginning to land on his left hand and bees are now landing on his right hand until there are six butterflies on his left hand and seven bees on his right hand. Cougar is not stung. He has become One with the bees as Grand-Pa had hoped.

URIAH HEEP plays: "He was the wizard of a thousand kings."

Cougar has furthermore become One with Everything around him. The Sacred Mountain guided this event...A purple plume explodes off the summit and travels into space. Night falls and the stars wheel across the sky. We see an eagle fly down from the sky. Its eyes get larger and larger until they take up the whole visual space and penetrate through until all is black.

                    COUGAR (CONT'D)
          {Whispers} Grand-Pa.

Grand-Pa's voice is heard from THE DEEP:

                    GRAND-PA ROBERTS
          Continue the next wave... You have
          our Blessings, my Son.

URIAH HEEP Wizard: "He had a cloak of gold and eyes of fire, and as he spoke I felt a DEEP desire, to free the world of its fear and pain, and help the people to feel free again."

INT. MIKE AND GINGER'S HOUSE - BOULDER - 1988

Cougar and Mike are sitting in the living room. Ginger is in the kitchen looking for something to do just to have some time alone. We hear plates clatter a little too loudly. Her frustration can be heard in the other room as she talks to herself.

> GINGER
> I miss Kathy... why did she have to leave us like that! So long ago... So long ago!

> MIKE
> Don't worry about Ginger. We have been going through some intense times, so when you come out with this story from Hell, it's just more than she needs to hear right now.

> COUGAR
> I'm sorry about that. I didn't expect a reaction of fear from her. I guess the power of just talking about something so Dark is disconcerting.

> MIKE
> We still have some catching up to do since you moved back to Boulder.

> COUGAR
> I certainly say so, Mike!

> MIKE
> And I've been meaning to ask you more about these Beings of Light in your Journey to Heaven.

> COUGAR
> Shoot!

> MIKE
> Did they tell you who they were? Their names?

> COUGAR
> They saw no reason to announce since I was given direct impressions of their essences.

> MIKE
> Like what?

COUGAR
Each one was a definite, unique power unto itself yet they were all tied to the central one, like that One was the summation of them all.

MIKE
The reason why I ask is because I went to one of those Revelation Revivals out of curiosity and they talked about the Seven Lamps of Fire Burning Before the Throne, which are the Seven Spirits of God. This sounded like your experience.

COUGAR
Very good analogy!

MIKE
And also Revelations mentions "Seal up what the Seven Thunders have said and do not write it down." All this talk of the Seven Thunders reminded me of what you were talking about, the thunderous Huuu you heard and how each voice was a thunderous peal of spoken Wisdom.

COUGAR
"Do not write it down." Times have changed. The world is more Enlightened because I am not only allowed to "write it down," I am allowed to talk about it without being burnt at the stake... But we just barely passed the days where they throw you in the nut house!

MIKE
No joke!

COUGAR
I met old Sister Thedra on The Mountain, the spiritual leader of the Great White Brotherhood. She told me her own family got her committed for insisting she spoke with Angels.

MIKE
Imagine that!

They both shake their heads in wonder.

MIKE (CONT'D)
This "Enlightened" Age, my foot!

They both have a laugh.

MIKE (CONT'D)
And then the Pastor mentioned Abbott George Burke claiming that "He who knows the Seven Names of the Seven Great Thunders wields the Seven Powers of God."

COUGAR
Ha! Who wants that responsibility? I got enough on my plate.

MIKE
Thought I would ask! Just wondering what you, or I for that matter, are capable of!

COUGAR
Funnnie!

MIKE
You are a rare bird, Cougar, and I like you for that.

COUGAR
Well, I would feel awkward telling anyone else this but you... The Seven Thunders told me that names are not important. Their messages were... Yet, I still could not help but naming them by their energy... This still sounds lame saying this...

MIKE
{Encouragingly} Go ahead!

COUGAR
The Thunderous Being in the center seemed to be the total Wisdom and Compassion of the Seven.

MIKE
Wow!...

COUGAR
One shone of Fidelity, very pure. One shone like a Lion, full of Courage.
(MORE)

                    COUGAR (CONT'D)
One was shining like an Eagle, with
an intense Focus, very Diligent.
Then Equanimity. They all shone of
Great Boundless Love.

                    MIKE
Wow! What if they are US at our
best? A shining example! What
power! Divine power! It is ours
too!

                    COUGAR
Who wants Power, anyway? Great
Spirit has the Power... Hell, even
Darkness has Power. I know that for
nuthin'... All I want is Ultimate
Truth! I won't be happy until I
have Ultimate Truth! I get sick of
these lies strewn all around us
like sweet candy.

                    MIKE
You know, I've heard that Truth is
not a flower to be plucked, but a
mountain to be climbed!

                    COUGAR
That's it, Mike! Yes! The risks are
great but so are the hard won
rewards... But... results are never
what we expect them to be... never!

INT. COUGAR'S HOME - MICROCOSM TO MACROCOSM

Cougar is sitting in the middle of the livingroom floor in
lotus position. His hands are on his knees palms down. He is
breathing rapidly and DEEPLY and then holds his breath.
The clock shows 5 p.m.

We see his mind go into his blood stream. We see his mind go
into his nervous system. We see his mind go into his organs.
We see his mind go into his head.

A calendar on the wall in front of him shows a picture of a
white pillar and a black pillar, symbols of Duality. A dragon
fly perched on the calendar, flies off into the air, across
the room and lands on Cougar's forehead. It sinks into his
forehead. Cougar calmly breathes out at 5:10 p.m.

Inside Cougar's head we see a beautifully vibrant green lotus
with a hollow center not unlike the iris of a human eye. The
background field is blue around the lotus and blue in the
center as well.

Cougar is seen moving into the familiar Third Eye of his meditations and investigates it really being a Star Gate. For the first time, he passes through it into another space!

Cougar sees a microcosm of forms that appear to be like blastulas or living cells dividing and multiplying.

Cougar moves beyond this scene and into DEEP space. Galaxies are seen swirling. Some galaxies are entwining with each other. Explosions occur. Now we come to star nurseries and dwarf stars.

Cougar flies past this scene and into the red, radiant cosmic background field. Cougar is at the beginning of the Universe. He passes through this field into pure white space.

A golden trumpet comes floating into view. Standing on the flared bell of the huge trumpet is an Angel of dazzling brilliancy. Gabri-El floats off the trumpet and puts the stem to his mouth and blows a mighty sound. It is a sound calling for the End of the World. Everything reverberates with its majestic sound.

Cougar can see the daily cycle of his own life surrounding him. He sees the karma, he sees the limitations, he sees the hours in sequence.

Cougar is whirling in the Dance of Life. Many chords are spinning out of his body into all of life around him. Many chords are as fine as spider webs. Some are larger chords that connect to the more important parts of his life, like Mike and Ginger. Cougar is floating in the middle of all this. He looks around himself, perplexed.

      COUGAR
I thought I stopped most of my games... my spinning of Karma... I want Ultimate Truth! Not Eternal Spinning of Illusion!

Cougar raises his arms and starts slicing with his hands through the fabric of Life until he tears it asunder much like one would a spider's web. Loose ends of the chords of light dangle everywhere in disarray.

      COUGAR (CONT'D)
Freedom! At last!

      GABRI-EL
Yes, you have freed yourself of incarnate life. You are Immortal. But to stay in the physical universe, you must dance and whirl like all others do.

The Angel disappears and Cougar is left alone holding the loose ends of many chords in his hands.

> COUGAR
> Oh no! What have I done? I meant to just stop the dance, not to exit life! I can't heal this by myself!

A black hole opens within his body. Cougar's skin is the Event Horizon of the black hole. He is being sucked down into the darkness. The mighty trumpet had called the End of the World alright... The End of Cougar's World.

EXT. COUGAR'S HOME

7 p.m. Mike and Ginger are knocking at Cougar's door. There is no answer. Mike looks in a window.

> MIKE
> My God! Cougar is slumped down on the floor! He isn't moving!

Mike finds the door unlocked and they both enter and rush into the living room.

> GINGER
> Cougar? Are you alright?

> MIKE
> Wake up, Cougar! Wake up!

> COUGAR
> {Weakly} Whaa...?

> MIKE
> Ginger, help me get him to bed!

Cougar is responding a little as Mike and Ginger help him to the bedroom. They put him down on the bed and Ginger pulls a cover up most of Cougar's body.

> GINGER
> Cougar! Cougar, are you sick? Mike, we should get him to the hospital.

> COUGAR
> No.

> MIKE
> Are you alright?

> COUGAR
> No.

                    MIKE
          What is it? How can we help?

                    COUGAR
          Black hole... Catatonia... Devil's
          darning needle...

                    MIKE
          Devil's darning needle?

                    COUGAR
          Dragonfly... Chords... Undone.

Cougar passes out.

                    GINGER
          Dragonfly? Mike, he's not making
          sense.

Mike and Ginger wait around for a bit.

                    MIKE
          Maybe we should just let him sleep.

                    GINGER
          Let's stay awhile longer. I'm
          worried for him.

Cougar hears them talking and tries to raise his head.

                    COUGAR
          Absolute...

                    MIKE
          What was that?

                    COUGAR
          Ultimate Truth...

                    MIKE
          What are you saying?

                    COUGAR
          The Ultimate Truth... is... Love.

Mike and Ginger look at each other, not **really** seeing the profundity of Cougar finally shifting to that place, to begin to really live it. Acknowledging Universal chords of Love.

                    COUGAR (CONT'D)
          Love... how did you know... to come
          by?

                        GINGER
            A strange thing. We both had an
            empty feeling in our guts like
            something was missing. We thought
            of you and just had to come by. Now
            it makes sense.

Cougar smiles contentedly.

                        COUGAR
            Yes, it does... You felt our chords
            loosening... disappearing...

Mike and Ginger look at each other, perplexed all over.

EXT. NATIONAL FOREST - COLORADO - 1990

We see a circle of around 25 people in a mountain clearing. Most are sitting on individual blankets. All are in comfortable clothing for dancing with maybe a few dance ornaments, nothing elaborate.

                        TOM WING
            It's true a Long Dance can get kind
            of tedious and tiring. But if you
            concentrate on the benefits, you
            will be alright. A transformation
            of any sort is worth the trouble.
            Sit out and rest anytime you seem
            to be up against a wall... Or shift
            from the Yang circle into the Yin
            circle... But often just staying in
            the same circle can bring on Bliss.
            Has anyone here experienced Bliss
            in their lives?

Cedar and Trish, who are both in their early twenties, look at each other and then at Jim.

Jim {38} is looking at Heather {40} with a range of expressions between Lust to Holy Adoration.

Cedar and Trish look back at each other with a mock disdain for Jim. Then they giggle.

About five people have raised their hands to Tom's question, including Cougar.

                        TOM WING (CONT'D)
            Very Good! That's about a quarter
            of us.

> QUESTA
> Tom?

> TOM WING
> Yes, Questa?

> QUESTA
> I have to say my Bliss has been very fleeting... and rare, but when it comes, it's beautiful!

Some of the others nod their heads. Jim is still staring at Heather. Tom acknowledges Questa's comment and continues.

> TOM WING
> How many people here have experienced Peace in their own lives?

Only Cougar raises his hand and when he notices this, he pulls his hand down quickly, hoping that he wasn't seen.

> TOM WING (CONT'D)
> Cougar, would you like to share?

Too late... He got caught! But he stays true to himself.

> COUGAR
> I experienced Peace over a decade ago when I was with the only woman I ever really loved. She brought me Peace for the five years we were together. She took it away with her when we parted... I have not experienced a Peace like that before or since her being in my life. I have walked DEEPLY on this planet. I have flown far into the universe. But this place right here in the middle...

Cougar pats his chest at the heart level.

> COUGAR (CONT'D)
> I lost more than I realized when I lost her back into the busy-ness of civilization. I lost my Peace. I lost my Power. I lost my Unobtrusively Compassionate Love for mankind. I have been struggling with this ever since. Perhaps if I find the right person again...

                    COUGAR (CONT'D)
          but it must be complete sharing,
          nothing less will work. That's how
          DEEP it runs in me.

Hannah {55} raises her hand.

                    TOM WING
          Yes, Hannah?

                    HANNAH
          I have never experienced Peace in
          my life. My childhood was bitter.
          My adult life has been fraught with
          grief. How can I find Peace in
          that? Or from that? And Cougar,
          perhaps you are just remembering
          only the good times with her.
          Sometimes fond memories will do
          that to a person. We tend to forget
          the bad times.

Cougar shakes his head no. David {65} raises his hand.

                    TOM WING
          David?

                    DAVID
          I haven't experienced Peace either,
          but I hope to one day... and not at
          the edge of the grave, no siree!

Some gentle laughter.

                    HEATHER
          I can't speak for Tom, but we
          haven't experienced real Peace in
          our marriage. Maybe spurts of peace
          after some tension, but all
          relationships have tension.
          Relationships must grow and it
          takes both of us to be successful.

                    TOM WING
          Thanks for sharing that, Heather.

Some laughter over Tom's voice being under whelmed. Jim is still entranced by Heather. We hear low oooh's from Cedar and a quiet TMI from Trish.

Questa {30} raises her hand.

                    TOM WING (CONT'D)
          Yes, Questa?

> QUESTA
> I have never known Peace. I have always looked for it but I have never found it... It seems that relationships are not the way to Peace, either. At least not for me. Relationships have always been trouble for me... But Peace, somewhere? Sometime? I certainly hope so!

> TOM WING
> So no one else has found Peace in their lives but Cougar? Anyone else? Rajan? Alegra?

Everyone else but Cougar is shaking their head for a no. Cougar is stunned. This seems unbelievable to him.

> TOM WING (CONT'D)
> I have found times I felt at peace but I guess it wasn't really lasting Peace. Maybe an hour or two. Nothing like Cougar's talking about. But we can all hope, can't we? My hope is that this Long Dance and other dances that we weave in the future will lead to lasting Peace and Bliss.

Tom looks at the sun.

> TOM WING (CONT'D)
> Now we have about an hour to prepare for The Dance in whatever ways you feel best... Rest or meditate and collect your minds. Let us try to keep talking to a minimum so we can prepare. Only those with dance prep chores are free to convey what is needed.

The dancers stand up. They pick up their blankets as they go. Some are going back to their tents to store them.

Trish, Cedar and Alegra {45} are walking together.

> TRISH
> Did you see the way Jim was looking at Heather?

> CEDAR
> He has really fallen for her!

                    ALEGRA
          I think it's kind of creepy...
          He was staring.

                    CEDAR
          A man in love.

                    ALEGRA
          It's not so innocent, though. He's
          actually sleeping with her.

                    CEDAR
          No!

                    TRISH
          And she's a married woman!

                    ALEGRA
          The sad thing is, I don't think Tom
          even has a clue.

                    CEDAR
          Would you tell him?

                    ALEGRA
          No.

EXT. SACRED DANCE CIRCLE

We enter the middle of the Dance. The Grandfather Drum is sounding loudly.

Some dancers are exhausted and are moving slowly. Some appear to be dancing at a normal energy level. Some are sitting out for a few minutes as Witnesses.

Both clockwise and counterclockwise circles have people dancing in them. This is an energetic commitment.

One person is in the center but no one is staying in the center for long. It is open for individual peak needs.

Cougar, Jim, David and Rajan are the four on the Grandfather Drum. Jim, of course, is watching Heather dance every chance he gets.

Cougar is watching Questa, as he is becoming more interested in her dance energy... and of course, her beauty. He is the first to catch a mischievous glint in her eye.

Cougar sees Ella is the next to catch onto Questa's shift to playfulness. It has been such a tedious dance for many.

Linda looks from Ella to Cougar, who are both smiling, and then looks at Questa.

Linda picks up her pace. Questa is hot on her trail.

Questa is tracking Linda. Linda feigns a broken leg and Questa pounces on her.

There is no physical contact during this play. Contact is usually discouraged, so they mime a little story of struggle without touching.

They both fall down into the center of the circle. Both are exhausted.

Questa picks herself up and leaves the center.

Linda gets up and leaves the center.

Ella goes into the center for a bit to "Witness" the energy that is left.

Tom comes out of the dance and touches Cougar on the shoulder which tells him he is ready to switch off.

Cougar, glad for the break to either "Witness" on the outskirts or dance, moves back into the Dance.

He dances in the outer circle first. The sun moves.

Cougar shifts into the inner circle. The sun moves.

Cougar dances the center for a bit and collects the sun into his body and moves through its warm rays that waft down.

Cougar moves back to the outer circle. He sees this dance is different than all the other dances.

There is so little joyful exchange between others except for the "Questa stalking" that occurred earlier.

Cougar feels like people have distanced themselves from each other. We can hear these thoughts of his as the drumming fades in his head.

                        COUGAR
          {Thinks} Why is there no love
          today? Where has love gone? This
          was such a tight community before.
          It's not just me... It's the in-
          fighting. It's mistrust. It's anger
          from deception.

Cougar spots Jim spying on Heather again.

                    COUGAR (CONT'D)
          {Thinks} Sexual temptation has
          brought the House down. It is the
          same story as in the world below
          us. Nothing has changed after all.
          I thought there was hope... at
          least here with these healers.

Cougar stumbles and catches himself.

He dances a little more and stumbles out of the circle to the Witness area and collapses to the ground. He attempts a controlled fall, so as to not draw much attention to himself.

He doesn't notice that all eyes are drawn toward him even though they keep dancing. Since when does he stop dancing?

The drummers begin drumming slower and more powerfully.

Cougar lays on his back with his arms out.

                    COUGAR (CONT'D)
          {Thinks} I feel so alone. All I see
          is grief and suffering around me.
          No peace? No bliss? Love is gone.
          What is the use of being around
          anymore? I'm ready for Home.

Cougar's body jerks a little as he stifles tears that are starting to come.

A tunnel of multi-colored light descends from the sky and widens just enough to cover Cougar. No one else sees this tunnel but Cougar.

The Voices of the Seven Thunders speak.

                    SEVEN BEINGS
          We arrre come to take you Hohmme.
          Is thisss your sincere wishhh?

                    COUGAR
          Yes, it is. Take me. I no longer
          belong to this planet.

Three dancers inexplicably break free of the Dance and rush over to Cougar's body.

Young Dave grabs both his ankles. Ella holds down a wrist and a shoulder. Heather holds down a wrist and moves from his shoulder to his forehead to his shoulder with her other hand.

Several women begin singing to Cougar from the Dance Circle.

Terry walks over to Cougar while strumming a guitar he has just picked up. Where did that come from? A guitar? Never!

Sylvia comes over to Cougar's body and places her hands above his heart and his solar plexus.

> **SEVEN BEINGS**
> Knowww that if we take youuu, there is nooo coming back this timmme.

> **COUGAR**
> {Thinks} I understand. Take me... My dance friends: Thank you for unblocking the energy in my body. Now I leave... I love you all...

Sylvia removes her hands but no one else lets go of Cougar. They hold fast.

The drumming is still low beat and powerful.

Women are still singing in the Circle. Simply unheard-of!

All eyes are still on him. Cougar is still paralyzed and only looks straight up.

Cougar tries to speak but cannot.

> **COUGAR (CONT'D)**
> {Thinks} You can let go of me now... Really. Please!... What are you healers doing! I want to go Home!... You are keeping me from leaving, don't you see!

The Tunnel lifts off Cougar and starts to recede back into the sky. Tears begin to stream out of Cougar's eyes.

> **COUGAR (CONT'D)**
> {Rasps} Oh no... oh no...

The healers release Cougar and all the dancers move back into the dance except Heather. She stays to help Cougar to his feet.

Cougar reaches a hand up to the tunnel that is almost gone.

Heather grabs his hand and reaches for his body. He is weak but manages to get up with her assistance.

Like handling a drunk, his arm is flailing around her shoulder and she has an arm tentatively around his midsection trying to stabilize him.

Heather carefully moves Cougar back into the dance.

The singing has stopped and the drumming moves back to its normal loud intensity.

Cougar is moving slowly, still disoriented while trying to dance. He sees the illusion of the reality that the others think is real. His head is in the clouds.

          COUGAR (CONT'D)
  {Weakly} Ha, ha, ha, ha, ha.

Cougar gathers up his strength as his laughter grows. Heather begins to smile at him with mixed concern. She puts a finger to her mouth.

          HEATHER
  Shhhh!

Cougar tries to quiet down but bursts of laughter still bubble to the surface.

          COUGAR
  Ha! Ha! Ha!

The laughter begins to pain him so he holds his stomach with one hand.

Cougar realizes that he would be better off to stop laughing. It's serious now for his health and his sanity.

He laughs a few more times until he is finally able to rejoin the others in normalcy.

The dance shifts to a better energy.

Most everyone is smiling. They are looking into each other's eyes much more so than earlier. The heaviness has lifted off of them.

EXT. CAMP BREAKDOWN - NEXT MORNING

The last Talking Circle is over. People are taking down their tents and picking up any signs of litter.

          JIM
  For some reason it's always easier
  to take down a tent rather than put
  one up... That always butters my
  buns!

                    TOM WING
It's just a matter of getting out
doors more. Then it becomes a habit
rather than a chore.

                    HEATHER
I see it kind of like a Long Dance.
It takes a bit of preparation and
hard work at first but by the end,
the process is complete and life is
sweet for a while.

                    QUESTA
Speaking of the dance, this one
seemed a little harder to dance
than I am used to.

                    TOM WING
It wasn't too hot for you, was it?

                    QUESTA
No, that part of it was fine. It
was a trying time for me... I
couldn't relax into it until near
the end.

                    TOM WING
Are you okay with it now?

                    QUESTA
Yes, thanks Tom. My process doesn't
feel complete yet but there is
always another dance to work things
out.

                    COUGAR
Heather, I have a question for you.

                    HEATHER
Yes, Cougar?

                    COUGAR
How did you and the others know to
come to my aid yesterday in the
Long Dance?

                    HEATHER
It just seemed the natural thing to
do.

                    COUGAR
But how did you know I was in
trouble?
                         (MORE)

                    COUGAR (CONT'D)
          I moved away from the dance action.
          I wasn't making a scene.

                    HEATHER
          Well, to think about it, I have
          never known you to take much of a
          break, let alone lie down.

                    COUGAR
          The funny thing was, it seemed like
          you all made a bee line for me
          before I knew what was happening.

Ella overhears some of this and speaks.

                    ELLA
          It is funny how we all saw you at
          the same time and converged on you.

                    COUGAR
          I had wondered at the time if you
          all had become telepathic or was
          this rehearsed somehow.

                    ELLA
          I felt like you were being a
          gateway for something.

                    QUESTA
          That's an odd thing to say. I heard
          several people say that about
          Cougar, too.

                    COUGAR
          A gateway?

                    QUESTA
          Yes, the dance was difficult for
          more dancers than just me... They
          noticed after you went through your
          process, the dance came alive. We
          were a real community once again.

On hearing this, Cougar becomes more bold.

                    COUGAR
          Did any of you see anything...
          um... unusual when I was down?

Jim, Tom, Heather, and Questa are shaking their heads no.

                    ELLA
          Well, I did feel a good energy
          shift at some point, so I released
          you back into the circle.

                    JIM
          Ya, then you became your normal
          dancing self, a Wizard lighting off
          fireworks from the hilltop.

Cougar gives Jim a nod like, so, you of all people have
glimpsed into my dance energy! Cougar looks at the others.

                    COUGAR
          You guys must have anchored me down
          for 20 minutes!

                    HEATHER
          No, Cougar. It was more like an
           hour.

                    COUGAR
          An hour! No way!

                    QUESTA
          Yes, way!

The Women's Group giggles. Unbeknownst to them, they kept
Cougar on Earth with great effort! Grounding effort.

INT. MIKE AND GINGER'S BOULDER LIVINGROOM - JUNE 1997

                    MIKE
          So, Cougar, I can't talk you out of
          moving to the Pacific North West in
          September?

                    COUGAR
          Time to move on, Mike.

                    MIKE
          So that last encounter with THE
          DEEP really got to you!

                    COUGAR
          Well, I've had Death Experiences
          all across the Country and this one
          has magically thrown open more
          doors. I must step through and see
          what's next!

MIKE
My Death Experience took me through the Tunnel and shared Love with a big "L". I met loved ones from the other side like many Death Divers do, but never Mythic Beings dishing out future prophecy and all that!

COUGAR
You know councils with Mythic Beings are less likely, but the greatest gift... we ALL get...

MIKE
Immortality. We all had to die in order to discover our own Immortality... Or re-discover...

COUGAR
People struggle with hope and faith in a distant belief of a promised Immortality. The difference with us Death Divers is we experience Immortality first hand. We _know_ it in our Core Being. We _are_ it!

MIKE
Funny how the Highlander Myth isn't far off the mark. When Conner MacLeod died and returned, he discovered he was Immortal. The big difference between us and the Highlander is _we_ don't have to cut off someone's head to gather power. Our own healing brings power.

COUGAR
Yea, all that Hollywood swashbuckling stuff! Think of all the people down through history who looked externally for Physical Immortality like Alexander the Great and Ponce de Leon.

MIKE
Don't forget Gilgamesh, the earliest of the Mythic searches for Immortality recovered.

COUGAR
They all travelled to the ends of the Earth for special elixirs and exotic fruits. They were all looking in the wrong places!

Mike nods in strong accord.

COUGAR (CONT'D)
Where is the contemporary Hero who has discovered the secret to Immortality is Spiritual and not Physical? Where is that Hero who has claimed it into daily awareness other than Buddha or Jesus?

MIKE
Well, I think people shun any who claim we know. We are unpopular for it. It gives us an uncomfortable edge. We know what is hidden. MacLeod's own clansmen feared him so much for being different that they ran him out of town.

COUGAR
I also think Shallow Pool Splashers instinctively know they can make loads more money selling elixirs and horns from endangered species if they perpetuate the lie that Immortality is Physical instead of Spiritual. Greed, greed, greed!

MIKE
There is no "Hero's Return" today for DEEP SEA DIVERS. When a Hero returns, he is ignored at best. Most people seem to turn their backs and walk away with indifference. At worst they...

COUGAR
Ah! Yes! That must be the Mundane Wall of protection the Dark Great Grandfather spoke of... Many shun what challenges their own mundane truth. Many more react with anger and fear when it challenges their religion... Should we even try to cause the blind to see?

MIKE
I wonder if we didn't have a choice in this, either... Nature planned this. The DEEP planned this. We Nine planned this with THE DEEP!

COUGAR
I know! We Nine agreed to come down from Creation within months of each other in 1950... It had to be at least Nine this time because Nature knew One alone would likely fail the trials by Fire and Death.

MIKE
We Nine knew each other well from other Journeys down though Time... A new challenge called to us... We made a pact together to come down to make improvements in the Course of History.

URIAH HEEP plays Tales softly in the background: "We told our Tales as we sat under morning sleepy skies."

COUGAR
Our hearts were aflame with unlimited possibilities but Nature knew we would fall asleep when we enter the World through the Womb. We forgot our purpose and the Nine became a distant, imagined dream.

MIKE
Nature incessantly gives forth its best fruit to endure, to survive life after life in the face of constant death.

COUGAR
Nature knew she had to wake us up with Death... DEEP DIVING... Very risky. Where One alone would fail, Nine are together. She knew One or more would survive.

MIKE
Yes! So in almost dying, not only we rediscover our Immortality but we rediscovered who we are and what we came down to do!

COUGAR
Unfortunately, it is an abrupt way to rediscover and comes at a great price. Some of our close friends of the Nine have died and some are too incapacitated to Win the Prize, as the Highlander puts it.

MIKE
Ouch, Cougar! Impermanence bites sometimes.

URIAH HEEP Tales softly: "No thought of sleep ever dwells upon the wise man's mind. Some task or audience, stealing every moment of his time."

COUGAR
Too bad we all couldn't work together as a team. Nature kept us apart with all its twists and turns. Life is such an intoxicating drug that by the time we knew who we were to each other, our paths were already in motion.

URIAH HEEP Tales softly: "Thus we have learned to live while mortal men stand waiting to die! {Die!} How can we do what must be done, in just one short life?"

MIKE
At least we Nine were able to recognise each other's Immortality when we met. It's in our eyes much like the Highlander again, with the sensation of proximity...

COUGAR
Yes but, we don't get that cool musical pitch when it happens.

MIKE
Ha, ha. But the eye recognition is there, none-the-less. Beyond our nine, we feel it in all Death Divers we meet.

COUGAR
It's not often that we meet another Deather, but I have recently heard of a large group in Seattle... Death Divers of all ages.

MIKE
So that is where you met Anne?

COUGAR
No, I met her on Mount Shasta and it was instant recognition. I even felt a pulse of familiar energy go through me when our hands touched.

Mike gives Cougar a knowing look.

COUGAR (CONT'D)
No, Mike, it wasn't like that...
It was one of those accidental
brushes, but memorable energy.

MIKE
That's how you recognized her as
the missing Ninth one!

COUGAR
Partially!.. A 1950 Gemini who
embraced the Universe, she did...
She told me of the group in Seattle
and that I should come out.

MIKE
It looked for a while there, that
we would find all Nine in Aiken,
where I was born a 1950 Libra.

COUGAR
Aiken came to hold the Lion's Share
of us. She nurtured us in the ways
of THE DEEP South. Fate brought me
to Aiken at age five to meet most
of you. It was sobering that Mark
drowned at 11 and didn't return.

MIKE
Tom died of congenital heart
disease when we were 13. At least
we saw that coming... Still a blow.

COUGAR
I thought that was the last of the
tragedy until Jimmy's motorcycle
went under that Semi when we
reached 18.

MIKE
Another blow! We were down to Six
when we barely got out of High
School!

COUGAR
I discovered Nigel in England when
we were about 22. Potential number
Nine. No eye confirmation.

MIKE
You know Steve and Dandij were
overwhelmed with drugs by 35.
(MORE)

MIKE (CONT'D)
They lost our Vision and one has disappeared under Witness Protection.

COUGAR
That leaves Four of the Nine.

MIKE
Danny got struck by a truck in 1975 and I thought he was going to die from another event in 89.

COUGAR
You look like that would have been a good thing?

MIKE
Come on Cougar! You know what a pain in the butt he was!

COUGAR
He's our Spiritual Brother and I find I have to love him!

MIKE
He has so much trouble turning his Vice into Virtue!

COUGAR
That's what makes him interesting! He is really trying to put his best foot forward!

Mike doesn't look convinced.

COUGAR (CONT'D)
He has done a lot of good public service over the years. Lots!

MIKE
Dandij and I thought he was just blowing a lot of smoke and we told him so to his face!

COUGAR
He is still our Spiritual Brother and you know he remembers us before this physical life... The Light Beings will never let him forget!

Mike backs down with Cougar's good reasoning.

MIKE
Yea, well, I guess... he just has more difficulties to go through than us... and we have been through a lot ourselves!

COUGAR
You know the old saying, "In time, all things grow toward the sun."

MIKE
He is on the Cancer/Leo cusp and loves being center stage! But you are a straight up Leo born just after high noon! A Tibetan Tiger. Bright and shining fame is in your name! Yet you're virtually an unknown. What's up with that?

COUGAR
Astrology can't really cover me. I am what Grand-Pa called a Shield Jumper. I have been around so long, I have lived as all the Signs many times over... We shot through the portal of Orion... a different sky map... The Pleiads... Ages before.

Mike shakes his head and sighs, knowing the same himself.

COUGAR (CONT'D)
I am not looking for fame... My constitution is as a quiet prophet and not as a performer. People see Danny's big ego and some just write off everything he says.

MIKE
I don't know what to believe myself since I didn't dive as DEEP as you and Crowley dived.

COUGAR
My life gives credence to some of his Visions of THE DEEP.

MIKE
How can you, when he blows up his stories more and more every year?

COUGAR
All the more to lend him support. Not just for Danny but for all us DEEP Death Divers.

MIKE
Why try? I feel far too removed from the general public's understanding of us.

COUGAR
Your preaching to the choir! Not only our Immortality, not only our proximity to the Uncreated Creating but also the inexplicable Powers that come to some of us.

Mike gives an exaggerated paranoid look around.

MIKE
Sshhh! Quiet!.. The Man might be listening! The Government might try to use us for the secret military.

COUGAR
Ah, they haven't come for me yet...

MIKE
The release of The Fury in 1978 sure didn't lessen my concern.

Cougar laughs at this.

COUGAR
Yes, I almost forgot that movie! The government kidnaps psychics and turns them into weapons.

MIKE
I was paranoid for years...

COUGAR
Oh, Mike!

MIKE
Until my powers faded...

COUGAR
Then there's that, yes, fading with Time. But, I still had to use sheer willpower to stop my Kundalini from exploding out the top of my head!

MIKE
Are you talking about the time you were with Kathy and stuck your arm through the livingroom wall?

COUGAR
Oh, boy! Yes! I just wasn't psychologically ready. I was holding on by the seat of my pants! My molecular vibrations were out of control and must have fired Kathy's cellular messaging by proximity!

MIKE
I didn't know you could stop Kundalini once it triggers!

COUGAR
There was no 1974 training manual. I willed it for my sanity, my life! Fortunately, that liquid steel slowed to a stop at my heart level. The place of my motorcycle fracture. The Anahata Chakra.

Cougar has a twinkle in his eye and shakes his head.

COUGAR (CONT'D)
Not your casual dining room discussion...

Mike laughs heartily and slaps his knee.

MIKE
No one would believe us anyway.

COUGAR
Try believing this... You know Danny and I were born within a month of each other and went to the same schools together with you...

Mike nods.

COUGAR (CONT'D)
We had Death experiences within a year of each other, both being in September.

MIKE
Yea, I remember, a car plowed into your motorcycle in 1974, whacking your Anahata and Crowley was struck by a truck in '75.

COUGAR
We both surfed the tunnel and met with Beings of Light behind stretch lecterns.
(MORE)

COUGAR (CONT'D)
I saw each Being as a distinct Virtue. He saw them as distinct Emotions.

MIKE
I have known you were both given future prophecy. Given vividly, but not cast in stone.

COUGAR
We had an odd intersection there too. One scene came where I saw a man wearing a cowboy hat riding furiously on the range along with cattle and other men with rifles. I was placed right in the midst of all that dust, smell and noise!

Mike nods, trying to visualize the scene.

COUGAR (CONT'D)
This was the only scene in black and white emphasizing it was an old cowboy movie. My attention went to that one man again. He had "R.R." in pale red letters emblazoned on his chest... One Thunderous Being announced this man would become the President of the United States in 1980. I thought, "Who? Roy Rodgers? Ridiculous!"

MIKE
{Incredulously} Whaaat?

COUGAR
Danny was shown political cartoons of a cowboy actor and the initials "R.R." under them. He also thought, "Who? Roy Rogers?"

MIKE

Whaaat? You were both wrong! It was Ronald Reagan!

COUGAR
But, we were both right! We both saw "R.R."! We both saw an actor cowboy was to be President in 1980, six years before it happened! So, Science, explain that away!

Mike laughs.

      MIKE
  What's the mathematical probability
  for that in numerical odds? I don't
  think it can be measured.

Cougar looks sad and far away.

      COUGAR
  Mike, I am really going to miss
  you. You should come out once I get
  settled.

      MIKE
  Perhaps after I retire.

      COUGAR
  I heard the Enchantments are great
  to climb and Mount Shasta is much
  closer than Boulder.

EXT. MOUNT SHASTA - SEPT. 1997

We see Cougar getting a late September climb up Mount Shasta. This has been many years in anticipated return.

He feels a strong female presence on the Mountain, but thinks it must be the energy of the volcanic summit, Shastina... The One who called to him ten years ago while on the male summit.

Now it is an eager/meager 12 hours from Central Washington to Mount Shasta done in one shot. This climbing event marks the beginning of his future annual treks to this Sacred Mountain.

EXT. CENTRAL WASHINGTON - ENCHANTMENTS - JULY 1998

We see Cougar climbing the Enchantments with a new hiking friend.

Lightning announces their entry onto the steep Aasgard Pass climb. It strikes so close to Devin that he steps through a crack in Time and sees the Expanding Universe, speeding up Forever.

He recovers to Cougar's knowing eyes as they shelter for a bit under a boulder that is leaning against the base of the pass. No rain comes. Just that one thundering strike.

They continue the climb to the top of Aasgard and down past the beautiful Emerald lakes.

Lightning claps farewell as they descend the Upper Basin... No rain. No other strikes... like some kind of Mythic Aasgard initiation of a long awaited welcome and goodbye... not letting them soon forget.

Devin is so transformed by his experience in THE DEEP that he writes the ground breaking book, "Everything Forever."

EXT. MOUNT SHASTA - SEPT. 2001

Cougar finally meets the Female Spirit of the Mountain. He had been casually tracking her barefoot trail since 1997 with no success. She really has a female form, manifest!

They meet in passing a few times between climbs and returning to tents for the night. Conversations get DEEPER.

As he says goodbye for the year, they unexpectedly become intoxicated with each other's touch.

They end up hugging but he resists her insistence to stay. He must return to Central Washington.

One final contact is a first sweet kiss... almost enough to change his mind about leaving.

He tears himself away and she is seen almost literally floating off the ground as he drives away, causing him to think for a moment that she is really about to turn back into Spirit form, the Female Spirit of the Mountain.

Sari finishes the painting she has worked on for over a decade and leaves The Mountain, never to return.

INT. COUGAR'S DREAMSCAPE - 03/03/2003 - EARLY MORNING

Cougar is sitting alone at a rustic table eating a meal. There are other tables in the middle of the room.

We see men at the bar and realize this is a tavern. The place has an Old Western feel to it.

Cougar, all of a sudden, becomes aware of himself in the dream, and expresses out loud:

                    COUGAR
            What am I doing here?

He stops eating and looks around at the tables and at the beer infested bar. He stays alert.

                    COUGAR (CONT'D)
          Ahh! I am in a dream! Hungry, huh?
          Let's have an adventure!

Cougar stands up and slaps a twenty on the edge of the table. As he is walking toward the front door, several men walk in, talking.

                    MAN ONE
          Yeah, she's a slut alright.

                    MAN TWO
          But she looks like a goddess.

                    MAN ONE
          And she puts out like a whore.

                    MAN THREE
          No, she's worst than a whore! She
          gives it all away for free. At
          least a whore charges something!

                    MAN ONE
          Nothing free about that! She can
          really cost ya if you don't watch
          out.

                    MAN TWO
          At least she is honest and up front
          about who she is.

Cougar pushes past these dream men, casually wondering what he is missing, but he is a man on a mission. No distractions.

Cougar walks outside and down into the street. He looks around him and upward, still awake in the dream.

                    COUGAR
          Explore or fly? Which is it?...
          Fly!

Cougar squats to initiate a jump into flight but hears a woman's lilting voice calling from an alley.

                    MYSTERIOUS WOMAN
          Cougarrr.

Cougar freezes, intrigued by the familiarity of the voice.

                    COUGAR
          Kathy? Is that you?

                    MYSTERIOUS WOMAN
          Come hither, my darling Cougar.

Cougar strides over and into the alley, excited at the prospect to meet his love from beyond the grave.

                      COUGAR
         Katherine?

He sees a woman standing in the alley with her back to him. She has long blonde hair like Kathy's hair. Flowers are woven into those lovely golden strands.

She spins around to greet him. She looks much like Kathy but she is not. She is in her mid-twenties. She is not quite beautiful but she is not plain, either. She looks like a wandering waif and is also very sensuous.

She is smiling, her eyes are hypnotic. She is wearing billowy silk genie pants, light forest green in color.

Her naked mid-section is showing her delicate and strong features, both from her spine and now her belly button.

Her top is bluish white, like the sky. This top is cotton fabric with long billowy sleeves.

There is an "Infinite Mandelbrot Set" design along the edges of her blouse, drawn in delicate black paisley curves.

The mysterious woman begins sauntering toward Cougar with great sexual power and charisma.

                    MYSTERIOUS WOMAN
         Those men are such fools. They
         don't know me!

She casually puts her arms around his neck.

                  MYSTERIOUS WOMAN (CONT'D)
         But you do, don't you?

                  COUGAR
         You are not Katherine. Who are you?

She slowly and sensually gyrates her hips, moving her body closer to his.

                  MYSTERIOUS WOMAN
         Dance with me, I know you want me.

Cougar moves his head back just enough that she cannot plant her soft kiss on his mouth.

She doesn't miss a beat. She moves her lips down to his neck and lightly tongues it.

> COUGAR
> I know you! You are like a sister to me... not a lover.

> MYSTERIOUS WOMAN
> Come on, sweetheart. Be mine.

> COUGAR
> I am yours! I feel your vulnerability.

The mysterious woman pulls her head back far enough that their eyes meet again.

> COUGAR (CONT'D)
> They know not what they do to you!

We see a fertile egg move from her forehead and into his head, much like the moon glow as it sets behind a mountain.

Then comes the "Infinite Mandelbrot Set" patterns out of her head, weaving and twisting into his.

They move apart, hand in hand, arms locked out. Their eyes are lost in each other's gaze, swimming.

> GAIA
> I am Nature, the Seduction of Life.

> COUGAR
> Mankind seeks to destroy you.

> GAIA
> Good! Gaia understands... Cougar understands.

Gaia straightens up and separates herself completely from Cougar.

Her energy shifts from Seduction to Inspiration.

She takes him regally by the hand and leads him down the alley.

> GAIA (CONT'D)
> I am your guide now.

> COUGAR
> Oh, God! The Great Spirit sent you to me, didn't He!

> GAIA
> Shhh! I will take you along secret pathways few men have ever been.

The couple come out of the alley and into the forest.

She lets go of his hand and walks swiftly in front of him for a time.

She stops abruptly. She points ahead.

    GAIA (CONT'D)
 It is time. Get thee in front of
 me, Cougar.

Cougar moves in front and the couple is moving slower this time. Cougar is looking intensively around.

    COUGAR
 Where are we going?

    GAIA
 Do not look back... Trust me.

Cougar does not look back.

Gaia's arms are out away from her sides a foot or so as they walk. Her billowy sleeves are flowing with every stride. Her footprints turn into little pools of fire.

With her hands out from her sides, everything on her right starts growing at tremendous speed while everything on her left starts withering and dying.

A large Temple is peeping out from the trees. The Temple is gray-green castle rock and partially covered in ivy.

Soon they are in the small clearing.

    GAIA (CONT'D)
 Continue.

    COUGAR
 What is this place?

    GAIA
 This is a Temple few men have seen.

Cougar turns around. His eyes get wide as he sees what has happened behind them. Then he looks into her eyes.

    COUGAR
 Enter it?

    GAIA
 Yes... Now.

Cougar gives a great tug and pulls the large creaky wooden doors open. They enter and the doors close behind them.

The reception area is the only area well lit. It is a huge domed hallway. Beyond that is a larger domed chamber.

There are a couple of monks in robes at the far end of the domed chamber.

Soft Gregorian chanting can be heard in the distance.

Gaia places a hand down toward Cougar.

              GAIA (CONT'D)
  {Lowered voice} Stay close.

They both walk casually along the right side of the chamber. When she is sure no one is watching, she ducks into the darkness of the space between the huge pillars and the wall. Cougar reacts quickly to do so as well.

Gaia is feeling the wall with one hand... She stops.

Click. A latch has moved.

She pushes open a small door leading up some winding stairs that continue on the inside of the chamber wall.

              GAIA (CONT'D)
  {Whispers} Follow me.

              COUGAR
  What is this?

              GAIA
  This is a place no man has
  discovered on his own.

Cougar follows Gaia up the dark stairs to the top.

Finally, a door appears on the left. It opens by itself.

Gaia remains on the stairwell and shows Cougar the holy room with her hand.

              GAIA (CONT'D)
  The Gods rejoice!

Cougar smiles at her and kisses her on the cheek.

He turns and enters the sacred room. This room must be at the apex of the huge dome below.

Gaia closes the door behind him and glides back down the stairs and out of the Temple.

Caravan of the Soul music is lightly playing.

On the light blue walls are many symbols and rare quotes in languages such as Ancient Sanskrit, Arabic, Hebrew, and Tibetan.

The top third of the walls are overlaid with woodcut forms in Arabesque that dazzle the eyes with their intricacy.

Persian carpets cover the floor.

Cougar is near the wall to the right.

The main section of the room is hidden by a seven foot high partition which is carved in Arabesque as well.

Cougar walks slowly to the edge of the partition where the main room begins to come into view.

>   GODDESS
> Welcome! We have been waiting for you, my dear Cougar.

Cougar leans forward, peering in as he enters the room, cautious with what he might discover.

He begins to see a woman with a solid gold ring resting around her long black hair. He braves in the rest of the way.

She is standing before a sturdy wooden table. She is wearing a gown of fabric which is glowing light green.

Six Children of Light float out from behind her in the air.

>   COUGAR
> You know me? {Bowing slightly}
> You have me at a disadvantage.

>   GODDESS
> You know us well, kindred.

Cougar looks a little dazed but starts to intuit.

>   COUGAR
> You Children of Light, look
> outwardly innocent, but I feel...
> I feel...

The cherubs move forward slightly and float up and down, smiling. A single note of a thousand violins become audible.

                        CHERUBS
              Yes?

                        COUGAR
              Your looks are deceiving! You are
              the most Ancient of Elders!

                        CHERUBS
              We are the First Ones.

Cougar puts his hands together in front of his chin. He bows
slightly to them. He looks back to the Goddess.

                        COUGAR
              And you are close to my heart
              somehow. I feel it.

                        GODDESS
              I am known by many names but not by
              many hearts.

Her voice is firm and noble:

                        GODDESS (CONT'D)
              I am Aphrodite... Venus... Isis of
              Egypt... Goddess of Fertility...

Her voice gets stronger with each name:

                        GODDESS (CONT'D)
              I am Kamilah of Persia... Ishtar,
              Goddess of Love from Ancient
              Babylonia.

Cougar recognizes the name "Ishtar" and falls to his knees
with his hands still in front of his chin.

                        INANNA
              I am Inanna from Ancient Assyria
              and before the Flood... before
              cuneiform was invented... Before
              Love and Lust and my name defiled!

Her eyes are glowing.

                        INANNA (CONT'D)
              I am from Times long before Human
              History... Times of Compassion
              Lost... I AM THE FOUNT OF
              COMPASSION!!! Pure unadulterated,
              Stainless Eternal Compassion!

COUGAR
{Feels this in his very being}
My Goddess!

INANNA
My kindred, you need not bow before
me... Rise.

Cougar slowly stands and puts his right hand over his heart.

COUGAR
My Lady of Compassion, how am I
your kindred? I barely know Love.

INANNA
You are no stranger to Love... or
Wisdom! You survived the core of
the Dark Pit as I have. The Throne
Room! Few men can speak those
words, indeed!

COUGAR
By the Grace of the Uncreated
Creating and the Seven Great Gods!

Cougar bows again to the Six Cherubs, palms pressed together
and up to his mouth.

INANNA
By your own noble heart! Cougar!
That Uncreated Creating Power, that
which mankind calls God, did not
abandon you in that Dark Pit when
you cried out for salvation...
Neither did God rescue you.

Cougar puts his hands down by his side.

INANNA (CONT'D)
You saved yourself by the
unrelenting power of the Heart.
You would not compromise your heart
nor your very Soul... How could you
then die?...

Cougar shrugs his shoulders a little.

INANNA (CONT'D)
If you <u>had</u> given into Darkness, you
would have died! Darkness is a
living, walking, breathing Death.
How ironic, isn't it? You chose
Life by choosing Death.

COUGAR
But my heart is a mere candle held out to the Great Sun of the Eternal Love I have experienced in the Heavens. How could I generate a Love like that?

INANNA
Now that you have experienced the Great Mystery, the Eternal Flame that is Ineffable Love, you know what is possible to generate in the human heart.

COUGAR
But how is that possible in this Degenerate Age? The threat of Death is all around us!

CHERUBS
It must be done! Especially now. This is The Dark Yuga.

The cherubs float in closer.

CHERUBS (CONT'D)
Even as we speak, the Earth is turning to gaze directly into the Abyss! You were sent to the Pit as a final initiation with Duality.

The cherubs rise higher in the room.

CHERUBS (CONT'D)
Now, my child, you have been dispatched here by our will for a greater labor of love. The world needs brave hearts.

COUGAR
My body and my heart are only flesh and blood. What can I _do_?

CHERUBS
You can do much more than you know. Remember you are Immortal. But not by yourself alone. Your gifts are given to you by the Ineffable Uncreated Creating.

A cherub holds forth its hand. A golden "L" appears in the space between them as large as Cougar's hand. It floats across to Cougar and he snatches it out of the air.

                    CHERUBS (CONT'D)
          This is the most important gift of
          your time period.

                    COUGAR
          What is it?

                    CHERUBS
          It is "LA." A fragment of the
          Ancient Lyrical Sound for God.

                    COUGAR
          How do I use it?

                    CHERUBS
          As a key. It will unlock a door.

The Cherubs point to the Eastern wall. Cougar walks over to it. He searches the wall but does not find a door.

He looks back at the Cherubs.

Inanna points at the wall.

                    INANNA
          Look with your heart.

Cougar places the "LA" on the wall in different ways until it locks in place.

He turns the symbol with the flat of his hand. A small section, perhaps 20 inches in diameter, turns with a sandy grating sound.

That round section of the wall disappears to show a portal to the outside world.

Cougar peers through the portal and sees a Priest on the lawn performing a ritual with the Christian Cross.

In another garden area, a Rabbi is performing a ritual with the Menorah.

                    COUGAR
          What am I looking at?

                    CHERUBS
          The <u>way</u> you unlocked the East Door
          shows the Way to the Prophetic
          Traditions of Religion... Judaism,
          Christianity and Islam.

Cougar turns back to the Cherubs. Another cherub presents its hand. A golden "7" appears in the air. It floats across to Cougar. He snatches it out of the air.

                    COUGAR
     What is this?

                    CHERUBS
     "ILAH." Another fragment of the
     Ancient Lyrical Sound for God.

The Cherubs point to the North wall. Cougar walks over to it. He works with this key more deftly this time.

Another sandy grating sound is heard. That round section of the wall disappears to show another portal to the outside world.

Cougar peers through this portal and sees monks reciting the Mahayana Lotus Sutra in Tibetan. Others chant the Heart Sutra.

                    COUGAR
     What am I seeing here?

                    CHERUBS
     Unlocking the North Door in this
     manner shows the way to the Wisdom
     Traditions of Religion... Buddhism,
     Hinduism, Taoism.

Cougar turns to walk back to the Cherubs. Two more gold letters appear. A backward "7" and a backward "L."

The portals that were open come to a grating close.

All four gold letters float toward Cougar and hover.

                    CHERUBS (CONT'D)
     The Four Great Traditions of
     Religion have different ways of
     holding the same symbol...

Cougar reaches out but hesitates on which to hold first.

                    CHERUBS (CONT'D)
     They each have their own entry to
     the Uncreated Creating. But none
     hold the whole truth... They each
     have a fragment of the One truth.

                    INANNA
     Cougar, do you know the One Truth?

COUGAR
To understand the One Truth, I must
know each Tradition.

Cougar touches the backward "7" and his intuition comes back into play.

COUGAR (CONT'D)
The third is of the Ancient Gods
Traditions of the Western Wall.

Cougar touches the backward "L."

COUGAR (CONT'D)
The fourth is Gaia of the Pagan
Earth Traditions of the South Wall.

INANNA
What is the One Truth?

COUGAR
The One Truth...

INANNA
Hold them to your heart.

Cougar snatches the four symbols from the air. He holds them to his chest.

He holds the "7" out and then spins it upside down.

COUGAR
It has something to do with seven.
The Seven Above. The Seven Below.

Cougar walks over to the West wall. He holds them up as a big rectangle.

COUGAR (CONT'D)
Four Square Earth, no, that's not
it.

He holds the Four as "L7L7." They float in the air just before the wall.

COUGAR (CONT'D)
Infinity. No, that's wrong.

INANNA
Reach into your DEEP well of
Intuitive Wisdom. Follow no one or
no thing. Look only to your Self.
The One is there.

> COUGAR
> Not one symbol in four directions.
> It is four of the same symbols in
> one special combination.

> INANNA
> El... La... Sacred Everything...
> Sacred Nothing...

Cougar turns them all to sevens.

He connects the bases of all four together.

> COUGAR
> Of course! The Sacred Symbol. The
> Uncreated Creating Life! The Four
> Arms of the Seven Flames!

The Sacred Symbol clicks onto the Western wall. Cougar puts his hand upon it and attempts to turn it.

Nothing happens.

> COUGAR (CONT'D)
> {Muttering} Ancient lyrical sound
> for God. {Louder} La ilah ila al-
> Lah! {No Gods, just God}

A seven foot diameter portion of the wall begins to turn with a grating sound.

The Uncreated Creating sounds forth from THE DEEP, chanting into Time and Space, chanting outward Time and Space.

> UNCREATED CREATING
> Lo! He has recalled the Mythic Key!

The Seven cherubs and Inanna are very attentive.

> UNCREATED CREATING (CONT'D)
> He is the One who will unite the
> Four Great Traditions of Religions
> into One! Behold him, my Seven
> Channels of Light in the world!

As the large portal begins to open, the soft violin strain that has been playing all along turns into sounds of intense, almost angry bees. Who dares enter this Sacred Space?

Cougar fearlessly steps through the round portal.

The hum of angry bees now turns into a soft resonant "Huuu."

Cougar is now in a great semi-dark cavern.

The six Cherubs follow him into the cavern.

> COUGAR
> This cavern appears dark, yet I see clearly.

> CHERUBS
> What you see is the Darkness of the World. We are in the hidden world of God within the world of Man... Only here may we see the Light of Spirit working invisibly in the world.

Cougar is inspired by this great mystery and sees visions.

> COUGAR
> Here is where all injustice makes sense! All dichotomies resolve!

The Cherubs, like sweet Cupids, each manifest an arrow. They hold them out to Cougar.

Cougar takes each arrow.

> CHERUBS
> These arrows represent the Six Directions: North, South, East, West, the Above and the Below. The Six Great Powers... The Six Great Virtues.

Inanna gracefully walks into the cavern and hands Cougar a leather quiver.

Cougar places the arrows into it.

> INANNA
> This quiver represents the Seventh Direction. The Direction of the Heart. The one that binds the Six Virtues together as One.

Cougar shoulders the quiver.

Inanna now hands Cougar a staff.

> INANNA (CONT'D)
> This is the Staff of Wisdom... Your wisdom, hard earned.

Cougar stamps the staff. He examines the hilt and discovers it can be pulled apart, exposing a sword.

INANNA (CONT'D)
This is a long sword of great strength and power. It is hidden within your wisdom so that men do not fear you upon approach.

Cougar swings the sword deftly a few times in the air.

INANNA (CONT'D)
This is the Sword of Truth... The truth is not easily received. The sword cuts the illusions of life that mankind cling to so dearly.

He swings a few more times with even more focus.

INANNA (CONT'D)
The sword cuts away the ego if false pride or false humility is held too strongly within them... Mortals curse the Sword of Light as it swings in their direction.

Cougar takes a couple more swings. He is moved by its power.

COUGAR
As the sword dances in the air, the sword sings dreadfully to some and to others, ecstatically.

He sheaths the sword into the staff.

INANNA
Yes, the sword is a true blessing for those who have faced themselves and conquered themselves... That wielder then understands everything at once with the touch of the sword, separating wheat from chaff.

Cougar tamps the staff twice to ensure its seal.

INANNA (CONT'D)
Critical decisions along the True Path of Life are made upon each song sung by the Sword of Truth during its to-and-fro motion.

The cherubs take the lead into the cavern. Their light becomes Cougar's light... They walk for a time.

Inanna is trailing behind.

> COUGAR
> Inanna, why do you stop?

> INANNA
> This is as far as we go... The rest of the journey is yours, and yours alone.

> COUGAR
> What do you mean? This is a maze of various routes. How will I know I won't be lost forever?

> INANNA
> Take off your shoes.

Cougar does so.

> COUGAR
> The rock is wet.

> INANNA
> We have explored these paths down through the Ages.

Cougar looks around, tentatively.

> INANNA (CONT'D)
> The path for you is sprinkled with the tears of Compassion from the Angels... and with the tears of the toils of Man.

Cougar glares back at Inanna.

> INANNA (CONT'D)
> You are standing on our shoulders until you feel the tears dry up. After that, the rest of the journey is your own personal story.

His shoulders noticeably fall to the new weight.

> COUGAR
> Don't leave me, Lady of Compassion! I am so weary of feeling alone in all of this!... This cold, Dark world of human suffering!

He looks so sad...

> INANNA
> Alone? {Gentle laugh} It was I who led you to rediscover the Seven Rings in your youth!...

Cougar knits his brow as he takes this in.

> INANNA (CONT'D)
> It was I who restored the Seven Meh, the Ancient Powers in your Seven Rings.

Cougar looks astonished.

> INANNA (CONT'D)
> It was I who guided the spinning Golden Ring into your hand as you journeyed into the Heavenly DEEP.

Cougar is speechless, his mouth agape like a stone Zardoz.

The Cherubs are so happy to gift him generously as well.

> CHERUBS
> You never were alone or lost... We will guide you in Dream Visions and place signs along the way... even more so, since the fall of the Twin Towers, presumptuous Golden Age.

Cougar gains a new strength from all he has heard.

> COUGAR
> I see what you know! The Wandering Sage, Al-Khadir, passed nearby ages ago. Moses walked with him for a day. You guided them, too!

> CHERUBS
> Because they opened their hearts.

> COUGAR
> I will miss you.

> INANNA
> You are only one breath away.

Inanna and the Six Cherubs fade out of view.

Cougar sighs and looks around him. He continues down the path. His feet are feeling the wetness of the rock.

As he travels, his body feels a strange yet, familiar wonder and awe. It is as if he has been here before.

It is like a forgotten dream from his childhood, partially emerging yet, out of reach... and intoxicatingly real.

This is an enchanted pathway that tells secret stories of Old and New as one travels through.

TANGERINE DREAM is playing the last 105 seconds of Cloudburst Flight from a 7:21 minute instrumental on "Force Majeure."

When Cougar spies civilizations on either side of him, he instinctively knows to pass by, quietly unnoticed. He is releasing the strange yet, somehow known attachments to the lands and places around him because the secret path itself is even more intoxicating the further he explores.

He instinctively knows the way without any doubts because of those changing body feelings as he goes. It is almost like an old young friend is with you, encouraging you to come back through the adventure, reliving untold forgotten memories.

Everyone must have at least one journey like this, from a half-remembered dream, illusive but so deliciously youthful and invigorating. A place we all but forgot that unlocks sheer joy from DEEP within. We actually shiver in the excitement of their return. A dream within a dream within realities. It is so healing and pure... And so missed.

The warm water flow finally dissipates to dryness.

Cougar stops to notice this and then boldly moves forward.

Down and down the trail goes. The world is passing by with vivid luscious greens of the forests.

At one point, Cougar slips off the side of the trail and falls into a giant pool of clear subterranean water.

He is submerged and going DEEPER. He kicks and fans to move upward but fails. He is so DEEP he has lost his bearings.

A giant Naga of Tibetan lore slithers into view. It comes face to face with Cougar.

Cougar looks astonished.

The Naga almost seems to be smiling. It telepathically speaks to Cougar.

>   NAGA
> No, I won't bite you.
>
>   COUGAR
> You can read my mind?

NAGA
Of course, Daka.

COUGAR
Will you eat me, then?

NAGA
Don't be absurd. I am your friend.

COUGAR
Friend?

NAGA
I forgot, Daka, you have the veil of another lifetime...

Cougar expels his air in bubble bursts while mouthing the words:

COUGAR
I can breathe!

The Naga looks askew at him and smiles. With its nose, the Naga lifts Cougar out of the water with ease.

The Naga pulls away and Cougar floats onto his back, suspended in the air.

COUGAR (CONT'D)
How is this possible?

NAGA
I offer you a precious jewel.

The Naga spits out a wonderful jewel which turns to ball-fire and goes into the seat of his spine.

NAGA (CONT'D)
I return a favor to you. You will need this in times of greater Darkness, looming on the horizon.

Cougar falls to the path he was on. He sits up and looks at the Naga with its head above the water.

COUGAR
I remember you, Aryaka. I will not forget!

He holds his staff in the air.

COUGAR (CONT'D)
I accept your dose of Kundalini, my dear Naga!

The Naga nods and tucks its head under water and swims away.

Cougar continues down the path he is choosing. He is almost glowing now. This feels like an all but forbidden path since no one else is seen on it in either direction.

Most others have no interest in travelling here, making it more wild, more sacred and most exciting.

TANGERINE DREAM starts 105 seconds into The Cliffs of Sydney with the drone chimes on the "Le Park" album.

Cougar is wanting to push through it to the end and yet, never wanting it to end. This is so delicious. He is honoring every moment, every change in the terrain.

Some signs of his future have appeared in the terrain, which are for future revelation in Angelic Dream Visions to come.

A bright point of light is shining in the distance.

                    COUGAR (CONT'D)
Almost out.

Cougar climbs down a drop off and further down to the end of the cave. He sees a sandy beach and a glistening sea.

TANGERINE DREAM seagulls are heard in Cliffs of Sydney as the song moves toward the end.

                    COUGAR (CONT'D)
The Sea of Mankind.

The Seven Beings Thunder Forth from THE DEEP.

                    SEVEN BEINGS
Sseeal up your exitt, lesst it be breached by the unnninitiated.

Cougar turns back to the cave and lets out a big roar in harmony with Cliffs of Sydney. A few pebbles tumble out.

Cougar holds out his right hand and roars again. Bigger rocks are heard tumbling in the cave.

Cougar holds out his staff hand as well and roars again, louder. A rock slide from the inside closes off the mouth of the cave. His quiver with arrows assimilate into his body.

Cougar turns to head across the beach to the sea. He spies a 70 foot ship close to shore.

A man and a woman are upon the shore. They wave to him and start toward him. Cougar waves back and picks up his pace.

They meet in the middle and shake hands and hug. They are newer friends not seen before.

> LORRAINE
> Welcome back to the Shores of Men. You look well!

> COUGAR
> I am well, Lorraine. I have discovered the Secret that connects all Men together, Religious or Atheist! We all move from Non-virtue to Virtue. Seven below and Seven above. Virus to Vessel.

David has an urgent look on his face.

> DAVID
> Time to talk comes later. We must board the ship now. Darkness is hot on our trail.

Cougar quickly adapts to the changing situation.

> COUGAR
> Then, let's be off, Dave. Good to see you again.

The three run toward the water. They climb into a boat and it motors away to the waiting ship.

Two security men who stayed ashore are being attacked by several evil looking men. They wrestle.

Four evil ones break free to come after the ship but are stopped by the men left in the remaining boats on shore.

The ship sails out with our trio on board and the secured boats follow.

The evil ones cannot swim fast enough to overtake anyone.

Our ship and boats pilot around a small island.

Two tall evil men dive off the island and swim toward the ship. They just don't stop coming!

They pull security off of the boats and into the water. They cannot be stopped. They are the strongest yet.

They reach the ship and climb aboard. Security on the ship cannot stop them, either.

David and Lorraine are standing behind Cougar on the ship.

                    LORRAINE
           How can we stop this Evil, Cougar?

The two tall evil men come right up to Cougar.

                    EVIL MAN #1
           We have you now.

                    EVIL MAN #2
           You cannot run.

Cougar doesn't want to run. He fearlessly stands his ground.

                    COUGAR
           And you can hide no longer.

Cougar reaches for Evil Man One's head and pulls off his human mask. Underneath, he is really a Daemon, black and red and bumps all over.

Evil Man Two sees this and fearlessly pulls his own mask off since they are now exposed. By doing so, they are showing how much of a threat they really are.

Cougar's words turn the cards on their fear mongering.

                    COUGAR (CONT'D)
           You are exposed.

The evil men are undaunted by his words.

                    EVIL MAN #1
           You will not complete your journey.

They lunge at Cougar.

Cougar confuses them by holding up a hand. They stop.

                    COUGAR
           Wait! I am honored you have come to
           challenge me. You both have great
           strength... Far beyond that of most
           men.

The evil men look at each other, surprised and suspicious.

                    COUGAR (CONT'D)
           We could really use your strength
           on our side. Would you join us?
           Shake up your programming? Shake
           off your conditioning! Vice into
           Virtue!

Cougar looks at them with so much compassion and honesty that it catches them off guard. They hesitate for some moments as they look at each other.

Then they finally nod to each other and look at Cougar.

> EVIL MAN #1
> We agree. No one's ever really given a rat's ass before.

Cougar claps him on the back and welcomes them.

The camera backs out and up and we see our beloved crew face outward to the open sea, full of new hope. The ship sails on to bright new horizons. Unity just may work after all.

INT. COUGAR'S BEDROOM {STILL 03/03/03} AFTERNOON

Robert Cougar is on the bed, eyes closed and unmoving. His face looks ashen grey.

The County Coroner checks his vitals. He looks over at one of the paramedics and says matter-of-factly:

> COUNTY CORONER
> Alright boys, you can have him. I am calling it now.

He checks his watch...

> COUNTY CORONER (CONT'D)
> 3:33 PM, Monday, March Third, 2003.

The paramedics take opposite sides of the bed and look down on him.

> FIRST PARAMEDIC
> Well, looks like he died peacefully. Sleep apnea, eh?

The second paramedic is intrigued by Cougar's salt and pepper beard.

> PARAMEDIC
> I bet he had a story or two in him! Too bad they will never be shared! The world will never know!

The goose bump ironic twist is he died with his story untold, yet we had the satisfaction of just now seeing his story!

A moment of pregnant silence. The paramedics lean in to lift him off the bed.

Cougar's body jumps unexpectedly, his eyes open wide! There is an explosion of a mouthful of air taken in. The paramedics spring backward, taken completely by surprise!

>   COUGAR
> I am not quite dead, yet!

Monty Python's Holy Grail reference is said tongue in cheek.

Cougar flashes back to the same explosion of air when he was eleven with his first NDE... his eyes are on fire with renewed intention, and now the next adventure begins!

EXTENDED ENDING

Cougar remains alone, without a mate, but not lonely.

Inanna of the Seven, the Invisible Lady of Compassion, slowly guides him forward. She is comparable to the Tibetan Tara, Bodhisattva of Compassion.

Inanna's Temple wall still stands today in Uruk. Her figure is in the wall, pouring life giving waters out to the inhabitants of Earth with the Tears of Compassion.

Enki of the Seven, Father of Compassion is recognized in Ancient Sanskrit as Avalokiteshvara, the Celestial Being whose tears of Compassion are as a life giving river pouring out into the World of Man.

He/she who is beyond duality, is tightly bonded with the Six companion Beings who promise Cougar signs and more Dream Visions since the disaster of 9/11 rocked the world.

After the Dream Vision with the ship sailing into the Sea of Mankind in 2003, the story picks up in 2007.

INT. MOUNT SHASTA CITY BOOKSTORE - SEPT. 2007

The Golden Bough Bookstore was established in Mount Shasta by Otto in 1986, a year before Cougar's first visit. This became his favorite bookstore for all of the mystical books it held. But he usually enjoyed sharing fresh mystical news more often than looking through books.

This visit, Cougar is talking to Jesse who is sitting behind the counter. She is dressed up today, inspired by a movie.

> JESSE
> It is so sad that my dad died with all of his papers unpublished. He was a brilliant man, full of creativity.

> COUGAR
> I feel for you. I have recently been saddened by contemplating how I might very well die before my unique adventures can be published.

> JESSE
> That would be such a waste!

> COUGAR
> They would be lost to the world forever! I am simply stunned.

A stranger walks into the Golden Bough.

> BILL
> Hi! I came in to interview for the Intuitive Healer program. My name is Bill, in from Sacramento.

> JESSE
> Hi Bill. Welcome! I am Jesse.

Before they can shake hands, Bill becomes enchanted.

> BILL
> This fellow looks interesting! Do you mind if I briefly read you?

> COUGAR
> You are welcome to try. I must tell you, I had two Palm Readers run from me when I was a young man.

> BILL
> Ha! I heard two Palm Readers refused to read Tilopa when he was young. They couldn't decipher him.

> COUGAR
> Tilopa, the Buddhist teacher?

> BILL
> Yes... Wait!... Huh! You are quite different than my normal readings.

Bill doesn't need his palm. He studies Cougar up and down, gazing at his energy. Cougar simply smiles.

                    BILL (CONT'D)
How unusual! You are concerned that
you have writings that may be lost
forever... That should not be a
concern. You are a Great Terton
Master from Padmasambhava's time.

                    COUGAR
Tertons are known to retrieve gems
or mind treasures from rock walls,
aren't they?

                    BILL
Normally yes, but you used to place
them into caves and rocks. You can
remember that talent and your newer
discovered treasures will never be
lost. They will be safe to draw out
in another lifetime.

                    COUGAR
I desire to aid people who cannot
think beyond the confines of mortal
civilizations and our accepted
reality. It is so limited!

The longer Bill looks into Cougar's Soul, the more emotional
he becomes. He sees some of what Cougar sees. He is moved to
shift from the comfort and control of opening others, to the
untested ground of opening up himself to others.

                    BILL
I am learning Compassion but I
struggle with allowing people to go
through the challenges they need.
It pains me not to intrude.

Tears well up and Bill begins to sob. Cougar knows his pain
very well and comforts the Healer with a hug.

EXT. MOUNT SHASTA - SEPT. 2008

Mount Shasta is going through many shifts and changes caused
mainly by visiting people from the "Civilized" World.

Cougar discovers a hidden cave that neither the Forest
Rangers nor the Native Elders know of, difficult to reach.

They have all heard the local legends of caves and magical
beings who live in the Mountain, of the rare chance
encounters with such beings and fantastic tales of UFO's.

Devas led Cougar here. He protects the cave's secret place.

EXT. MOUNT SHASTA - SEPT. 2011

The Cave draws Cougar DEEPER into its secrets each year. There is an exchange of Mountain and Man.

There is an uncanny peppermint scent that always greets Cougar to the cave. Sometimes it fades in a few minutes, sometimes it stays in the cave all day, like a Divine Presence guiding his practice of Compassion.

The Cave drew Cougar there to establish a spokesperson from the human heart to represent Man to the Mountain.

The Cave reciprocates this year with Visions of youth calling out. The 23 year old's of 2011 were 13 when they suffered the trauma of 9/11... just as Cougar was 13 when President Kennedy was assassinated in 1963.

Cougar understands that many of these youths have become seekers of positive change in the world.

He leaves the cave to engage them in heartfelt fireside conversations. This is the beginning of something wonderful.

INT. IADDS MEETING - SEATTLE - OCTOBER 2012

The monthly meeting of IADDS in Seattle is coming to a close. The International Association of Death Divers Studies.

It is at the end of the Q&A portion. Cougar is the presenter of the month. The host addresses the hundred people in the audience, many of whom are Death Divers themselves.

>							KIM
> We have time for one more question before we end for the day...
> Anyone?

>							QUESTIONER
> You say the Seven Virtues you describe in Heaven may be Seven Anunnaki. Are these the same Anunnaki of the planet Niburu who enslaved mankind to mine gold?

>							COUGAR
> You are referring to Zecharia Sitchin's work, whom I really admire for translating Ancient Sumerian texts. Through him I have found many realistic connections to my own Death Experiences beyond the scope of today's talk.

There is some encouragement from the audience to tell all.

> COUGAR (CONT'D)
> I must say I personally think the Anunnaki are more spiritual than literal... If one looks at the supposed orbit of Niburu being 3600 years and Pluto's is 248 years, how warm is our Sun? I think that by the time Niburu swings back closer to the Sun, all we would have to worry about is Alien Popsicles!

Audience laughter and the program ends.

INT. SEATTLE HOME - SAME DAY

Cougar is invited to dinner. Afterwards, the home host is googling through her computer while others chat.

> MARTHA
> Come here, Cougar! Take a look at this! This is just posted!

As Cougar walks over to her, she reads the headline.

> MARTHA (CONT'D)
> 'Iron Man' Buddhist Statue To Have Been Carved From Space Rock.

> COUGAR
> Oh, really?

> MARTHA
> The Buddha meteorite matches those found in the Chinga meteorite field. The estimated impact is around 20,000 years ago.

> COUGAR
> Wow! Nice carving, Martha...

Martha continues...

> MARTHA
> The carving depicts a man, probably a Buddhist God, perched with his legs tucked in, holding something in his left hand...

> COUGAR
> Looks like a fruit of Immortality!

> MARTHA
> On his chest is a Buddhist swastika, a symbol of luck that was later reversed by the Nazi party of Germany.

> COUGAR
> Zoom in, please! I can't quite see!

Martha enlarges the image until...

> COUGAR (CONT'D)
> I don't believe it! The God of the Four El's!... The Uncreated Creating! El of the Four Sevens.

> MARTHA
> You mean the Four Traditions of Religions! I see it!

> COUGAR
> What synchronicity!

> ANNE
> {Overhearing} Our future is yet to be explored and fulfilled!

EXT. MOUNT SHASTA CITY - 17 SEPT. 2015

The time is ripe for Cougar to be graced with meeting Jonathan. He is ushered into a house with pictures of a thousand other Saints all over the livingroom walls.

Incense and classical music softly penetrates the room.

Jonathan is sitting in a chair at one end. He looks to be about 63. He has a full head of wild blond hair, a long beard, divine smile and compassionate eyes.

Jonathan remains seated with his head slightly down when Cougar approaches. Cougar bows down on one knee to meet Jonathan's eyes.

Jonathan gestures for his hands. They hold hands.

> COUGAR
> I have been looking for you since I first heard of you on the Mountain over ten years ago.

> JONATHAN
> I know, my brother.

COUGAR
I heard you were a practitioner of Compassion there for 20 years. I wanted to thank you for all of those years of service.

Jonathan, with a twinkle in his eye, nods his head.

JONATHAN
I would break the ice in the stream in November to bathe.

COUGAR
I found a cave in 2008 that I suspect you were practicing in.

JONATHAN
That is the last year I was physically able to reach the cave.

COUGAR
So, I was led there to continue the exchange between Man and Mountain!

JONATHAN
Yes, my brother... before me was brother Haiku. Joshua Morrissey.

COUGAR
I just met him on the mountain in 2011! We spent 3 days together and he gave me an intense 3 hour mind transmission one day. He knew of the cave, but I didn't know he had been practicing in it...

JONATHAN
Yes, my brother... And before him was brother Ericks in the '70's.

COUGAR
Brother Ericks! I met him in 1987! I have run into him several times over the years, but he never told me about the cave!

JONATHAN
You were being prepared, but if you failed, you would never find it.

COUGAR
You three have had the most impact on me for memories of the Mountain!

                    JONATHAN
          There was a mountain lion in the
          cave before Ericks who raised its
          young there before they left.

                    COUGAR
          {Cougar laughs} And now it comes
          full circle with another Cougar!

                    JONATHAN
          Come closer.

Cougar moves to both knees and Jonathan motions him to touch
foreheads. Rainbow balls of light travel between foreheads.
A great mind transmission takes place.

Both men gently laugh a moment. Then a blinding white light
shines between them and both men move back to where they were
in the beginning, still holding hands.

                    JONATHAN (CONT'D)
          You are touched by the Angels!

EXT. MOUNT SHASTA HIDDEN CAVE - SAME WEEK

The day of the full moon, Cougar is practicing in the cave
when a crown of flaming clouds appears over the cave...
The Mantle has officially been passed!

Cougar is the guardian practitioner for now. It was all
synchronistically ordained. There is rare photographic
evidence that Truth IS stranger than Fiction!

EXT. MOUNT SHASTA PANTHER MEADOWS - SAME WEEK

Cougar is led by the Mountain to meet four scouts for the
International Rainbow Gathering passing through Panther
Meadows. JusOne, Beatrice, Megann and Jake.

The Mountain whispers for him to spend time with them as they
locate near the Pacific Crest Trail. The Cave is guiding
Cougar's intention request, "Where do El's teachings go?"

EXT. PACIFIC CREST TRAIL - SAME MONTH

More than 100 beautiful youths of many countries from South
America to Norway trickle in for this wonderful Healing
Gathering. J1 and Bea set up a "Tea Here Now" camp on a hill.

There is one main fire for food circles, singing, dancing,
laughing and musical instruments from guitars to Didgerydoos.

There are no drugs here, only intentions of healing. Cougar sees how this is in total alignment with the teaching that Cave Visions have given him of turning Vice into Virtue. One cozy night fire with almost two dozen beautiful International youths allows this Vision to be engagingly passed on.

On September 27th half the group go up to the ridge for three hours of silence as a rare sky event begins to take place. The other half stay down by the fire with instruments.

The Supermoon is in total lunar eclipse as it rises. Finally a little sliver appears and grows until the whole moon is shining brightly. There is some suppressed crying and laughing and a gentle guitar sound breaks the silence.

What sweet blessings to have stumbled into all of this magic. Who could imagine such fortune? True riches! Most certainly!

INT. SOUTH CAROLINA - FATHER'S AIKEN HOME - 6 NOV. 2015

Cougar is visiting relatives in South Carolina.

Father has gone to sleep in his downstairs bedroom. Cougar is reading a hundred year old philosophical treatise on life after death a dear old friend offered him while he visits.

Cougar finally beds down in the guest room upstairs but he cannot sleep. He tosses and turns for hours. He sits up in the dark, worried.

                    COUGAR
     Two in the morning? Why can't I
     sleep? What is this sense of dread?

He finally falls asleep but wakes again and looks at the clock.

                  COUGAR (CONT'D)
     Three? What is this sense of dread?
     It won't go away... I hope dad is
     okay, he just had his 88th
     birthday!

He ignores the urge to go down and check on him. He falls asleep but wakes again.

                  COUGAR (CONT'D)
     330? That's it! It's not going
     away! It's either me or my dad...
     I just hope he is okay!

Cougar cannot intrude on him unwarranted. He falls asleep but wakes to an Etheric Voice at four in the morning.

> ETHERIC VOICE
> We are having a meeting at 6 AM.

He drifts off again only to waken to the same voice.

> ETHERIC VOICE (CONT'D)
> Remember, we are having a meeting at 6 AM.

He nods off, a little perplexed. Then several voices wake him.

> ETHERIC VOICES
> We are all having a meeting at 6 AM.

> COUGAR
> {Mumbles} Alright, I won't forget.

One strong voice calls out.

> ETHERIC VOICE
> Meeting at 6 AM! Be there!

Annoyed, Cougar shouts out.

> COUGAR
> Alright! Alright! How could I NOT be there!? What is all this nonsense? Leave me alone already!

6 AM approaches and with it comes a vivid Stroke Vision.

Cougar is looking up from a dream field and sees a 747 tumbling out of control, nose over tail, uncannily slow, like huge objects seem to do in the sky. Death seems immanent.

> ETHERIC VOICE
> Do not move!

Resigned to the fact that he cannot move away in time, Cougar has a realization.

> COUGAR
> At least this dreaded fate is not for my father, beloved by many for his selfless caring service to others.

The 747 comes crashing down upon Cougar, flattening him to the Earth and disappearing.

Cougar is shown a natural hollow in his body where the 747 has flown through, only nicking a wing on the left side of the tunnel.

The scene opens to a hillside full of robed Beings. Some heads are hooded. These are Living Masters and Ascended Masters from ALL the blessed religions ever birthed on the Earth!

Some are praying with palms pressed together, some are nodding their heads as if they are greatly pleased.

> ETHERIC VOICE
> A great disaster has been avoided.
> Thank you brothers!

This is nothing short of miraculous, and many of these Honored Guests speak out in quiet exclamations of awe.

Then Cougar is addressed.

> ETHERIC VOICE (CONT'D)
> We spent decades carefully preparing you for a teaching. You passed all the trials. We move in Divine Will together.

Cougar looks at them quizzically.

> ETHERIC VOICE (CONT'D)
> By gathering here, we proclaim a vested interest in your attempt to bring forth that teaching and bless this moment to allow your physical continuation.

Cougar nods, still not really knowing what almost happened.

> ETHERIC VOICE (CONT'D)
> This Teaching is ancient and simple. All resonate with it. It embraces all religions. This is the purification of the Individual and Universal Mindstreams, so needed in these historically shifting times.

Cougar is back in the bedroom. It is indeed 6 AM.

He stumbles for the bathroom but his right side fails him. His words do not come forth clearly.

In the hospital, the Neurologist shows him through layers of his brain on the computer MRI in 3D.

As they approach the brain stem, she says this is the location of the damage. The top left side going into the tunnel shows a red mark. It is the area the Etheric Beings have shown him. A very serious location.

The first doctor surmised this was a major stroke but Cougar recovers quite a bit in the first week. A blessing, indeed! 747 size Disaster averted with invisible hands from THE DEEP!

INT. COUGAR'S HOUSE - MID-STATE WASHINGTON - MARCH 2016

Mike is visiting from Colorado after Cougar's stroke.

          MIKE
I see you still have no minstrels skipping along behind, singing new songs of Heroic deeds!

          COUGAR
{Chuckles} I think I would have tripped over them in my twenties and broken my neck... Then, where would I be?

          MIKE
I remember the good old days when you got me excited with the news of your Heavenly experience of the Seven Thunders...

          COUGAR
Who would not be named.

          MIKE
Then you called them Anunnaki.

          COUGAR
The 7 stars of the Big Dipper that never set! Today, I might call them the Seven Wisdom Dakinis.

          MIKE
What are Dakinis?

          COUGAR
Dakini in Sanskrit is literally, "Sky Dancer." They transform our mental poisons into Enlightened Awareness. Vice to Virtue.

MIKE
How apt! The Seven Deadly Sins turning into the Seven Heavenly Virtues, Tibetan style!

COUGAR
When Black Elk was only nine years old, he nearly died and was called up into the clouds to meet his Six Grand-Fathers. I will never forget Black Elk's words: "Their voices were very kind, but I shook all over with fear now, for I knew that these were not old men, but the Powers of the World."... The Six Directions. But they calmed him and told him, "We are you."

MIKE
So where is the Seventh here?

COUGAR
Ahh! The Six Grand-Fathers gave Black Elk a flowering stick and told him to plant it in the Center of the World... The stick would flower into a tree to shade and protect everyone. Here we go back to the Tree of Creation. The Tree of Life. Yggdrasil of the Norse. The Immortal Tree of various World Cultures... I could go on and on but you get my point.

MIKE
You do go on and on! But please do.

COUGAR
My Seventh was the total Wisdom of the Six. Were these Beings merely my Higher Self? I don't honestly know. All I know is that all Four Traditions of Religions recognize growing from Vice to Virtue. Virus to Vessel. This even includes Atheists who don't believe in a God or a Higher Self. They just want to leave the World a better place for their children's children.

MIKE
What else can we ask for? This is great stuff!

COUGAR
This is huge. We all grow toward being One, regardless of our Holy Wars... Territory... "I"-ness... Boundaries... Lack of resources.

MIKE
The Heart is a Flowering Tree.

COUGAR
The Heart is quite a Mystery to explore.

MIKE
Only for the Brave.

COUGAR
Only for the Brave of Heart.

MIKE
Ha!

COUGAR
And each one of us is like a Flowering Tree. A Tree of Life. Every branch from us connects to an aspect of life we live... The Antahkarana. Our light webs are those branches. Our light chords connect to the things we love.

MIKE
Who are you!
We are you!
We are One!
Wow!!!

Cougar smiles at Mike's dawning awareness.

COUGAR
Mike, have I told you about the Other Key? Gaia intoxicates us with puberty and we get stuck between survival and control. The Other Serpent in the Other Tree is the Key back Home... We all freely explore: Down the Tree of Duality then up the Flowering Tree of Life. Vice to Virtue. All is Ultimately Sacred.

Now comes a long pause, and then the silence is broken...

MIKE
Wow, wow... wow, wow, wow!

COUGAR
What?

Mike Points at Cougar's ring-less hands.

MIKE
Didn't you wear 7 rings back in high school?

COUGAR
Very good! How in the world did you remember that?

MIKE
{Thinking hard}
Remember Danny? Wasn't he envious of those rings? Something happened that...

COUGAR
I had a Dream Vision as a child that I discovered 7 rings at the bottom of the ocean.
{Staring intently into Mike's eyes}
I had placed those rings down there from a lifetime in Atlantis.
{Drawing Mike in with his eyes}
Those rings held the Seven Virtues, the Sacred Meh gifts of Inanna.

Mike's head involuntarily jerks back a bit as a tiny blue ball wheels toward his eyes from Cougar's eyes.

MIKE
What in the world?...

Cougar sees this, relaxes and smiles at Mike's reaction.

COUGAR
Oh, that! The Thigle!

Mike is stunned being caught off guard with the spinning ball, and now confused with Cougar naming it.

MIKE
The what?

                    COUGAR
          The Thigle. You know, the little
          balls of light I had been telling
          you happening between Kathy and I
          when we were much younger.

                    MIKE
          The Thigle! They are for real!?

Mike says this as a new undeniable discovery but still
questioning the fantastic nature of its very existence.

                    COUGAR
          The Tibetans have this recorded
          through the centuries as a passing
          phase while developing Awareness.

He says this matter-of-factly and then shifts gears...

                    COUGAR (CONT'D)
          Funny how I just discovered an
          ancient Tibetan prayer the other
          day which is used by people in
          daily practice:
          "In all my lives, whereever I am
          born, may I obtain the Seven noble
          qualities of the Higher realms."

                    MIKE
          If this Mind Training triggers that
          second dose of Kundalini from the
          Naga that found you... added to the
          first dose you were able to
          suppress...

                    COUGAR
          Yes, I am amazed at the stories
          that are now translated from Tibet
          on achieving Rainbow Body...
          accelerating molecular vibrations
          at onset of physical death...

                    MIKE
          Transformation! Transfiguration! It
          seems too incredible in our Western
          culture! Only Jesus was allowed...

                    COUGAR
          Mike! I've got to take you to meet
          some brothers and sisters at IADDS!
          I must give away The Core Teaching
          Of The EL-ders and then, perhaps we
          will restart the Sacred Drum Dance!
                    (MORE)

>   COUGAR (CONT'D)
>   The Dance that transforms Vice to
>   Virtue, Virus to Vessel!
>
>   MIKE
>   As you answer the call, the Angels
>   said you may be given more Dream
>   Visions to guide you safely.
>
>   COUGAR
>   Retirement is here! 51 years a
>   slave! Now is the time to do the
>   Real work and strive beyond Self
>   Actualization. The Naga dropped by
>   the other night! Our story has just
>   begun, not--"The End!"--Foolish me.

EXT. MOUNT SHASTA PANTHER MEADOWS   -   SEPT. 2016

Cougar establishes his base camp in Panther Meadows #6, a most popular private site, very difficult to nab. Every year he asks the Mountain and ALL the Heavenly Hosts to guide his footsteps to whatever and whomever for the highest good.

This first night, Kathy appears before him three times. She looks DEEPLY into his eyes for a long time each time, and each time without saying one word; a hint of things to come.

The next day a fire is spotted early by Amelia Rose down in #15, closest to the trail leading down to the sacred spring. At first it looks like morning fog. Then young Amelia can see it really is smoke and calls out.

Fifteen campers gather blankets and water jugs and run down to smother the fire that has spread through the root system to three 1500 year old Ancients. The fire is climbing the trunks fast. The campers act faster and put out the flames before the firemen can arrive. They call off the helicopters. We can feel the thanks and blessings of the Ancients. This is only the beginning of the blessings upon us.

Cougar hikes in DEEP, to the Sacred Cave. He experiences three full nights of Tummo, the inner heat that comes to sincere practitioners. Tummo is known to melt off snow and bring energy to the body for transformation. Then one night:

>   CAVE WHISPERS
>   Cougar, my son. You and the Indian
>   Saint Tilopa have discovered at an
>   early age that your True Parents
>   are not of Earthly flesh and blood.
>
>   COUGAR
>   {Whispers back} Yes.

                    CAVE WHISPERS
          A thousand years ago, Tilopa was
          given three parts of a key to
          unlock a Mind Treasure, offering
          pristine Awareness to others.

                    COUGAR
          {Whispers back} Yes.

                    CAVE WHISPERS
          Thirteen years ago, you were given
          four parts of a key to Unite All,
          slowing the shamanic dance of
          destruction between peoples.

                    COUGAR
          {Whispers} Yes.

                    CAVE WHISPERS
          For nineteen years now, you have
          faithfully shared your teachings on
          this Mountain and elsewhere.

                    COUGAR
          {Louder} Yes, but I tire with how
          slow verbal transmissions are.

                    CAVE WHISPERS
          Yes.

                    COUGAR
          {Louder still} It sometimes takes
          hours but over the years I feel
          empty when nothing DEEP is shared
          back to me! A lonely gulf remains.

Cougar's voice trails off. A long silence marks that gulf
once again. Why is that gulf so Vast? Mankind, where are you?

                    CAVE WHISPERS
          The time is ripe to test your
          readiness for transformation.

                    COUGAR
          Transformation?

                    CAVE WHISPERS
          Your genesis of transformation from
          storyteller to facilitator starts
          Now! Direct Mind Transmissions.

                    COUGAR
          Uh, oh... I mean, "Yes?"

> CAVE WHISPERS
> You will take others by the hand or eye, into THE DEEP, guided by the Uncreated Creating, Great Spirit and Light Beings of the Sacred Mountain of God, if you will.

> COUGAR
> I will... but how?... and when?

> CAVE WHISPERS
> You will know how, when we guide.

From now onward for most of the month comes only three to four hours of sleep each night. The rest is "work" and prayer and waves of Joy.

Cougar could easily see how blind people are to the Eternal Love that surrounds everyone ALL the time... It is hidden within them as well. He sees the loss in their eyes of a Love and Light and Sound they don't even consciously know exists! Everyone is stardust covered up by mud! Something must be done! Something much quicker and DEEPER than old stories of human potential. Cougar's saddened and moved heart prays:

> COUGAR
> Be with me now, all Buddhas and Bodhisattvas and all protectors of Virtue! Of the ECK and the HUUU and ALL the Spiritual Leaders that recently came to save me from my deadly stroke, to do the real work!

Summit climber Tony sees Cougar from his own campsite. Tony is moved to visit and gifts him a green Moldavite crystal.

> TONY
> This is from my hometown in Bohemia. It is from a singular meteorite 15 million years ago. It is the only meteorite to give olive green crystals such as these.

> COUGAR
> {Stunned} I am honored, Tony! I have been dreaming of this green crystal for decades. Touching it in my dreams foretold of lost power coming back to me from lost love.

> TONY
> The artist, mystic Nicholas Roerich called it the Agni Mani or Fire Jewel. I felt it call out for you.

After Tony departs, Cougar holds the Fire Jewel to his heart and prays:

                    COUGAR
        I cannot forget my friends! I call
        in more personal beings such as
        Cherokee Grand-Pa Roberts, Buddhist
        Intuitive Drew Daniels and this
        Mountain's own Jonathan River Wolfe
        who most recently passed away into
        THE DEEP!

A tear passes down Cougar's cheek from the recent shock.

                    COUGAR (CONT'D)
        All of you have gone to the Great
        Beyond! Be with me Now! Add your
        great Heart power to mine for the
        sake of ALL beings! Hear my plea!

Cougar carefully places the green crystal under his compact pillow as he beds down in his tent that night in Panther. He dreams that it burns a hole in his pillow at 168 degrees to align itself with him. It sears DEEPLY into his brain.

A mansion of many floors and many rooms appear. In each room of each floor, a smorgasbord of Spiritual Foods and deserts of all kinds await our traveller. Cougar is free to roam and sample the best of the best.

The next day, Cougar meets Rachel and Heather. He watches them feed and play with the chipmunks who quickly trust the sisters. Rachel actually strokes one on the belly as it grudgingly accepts in order to continue snacking on the chip she holds tightly in her hand. Ah! A reminder of Sari! The Original Sacred Female energy returns to the Mountain!

The next day, Cougar hears the Mountain whisper, so he leads Rachel to his campsite. They sit on the bare ground facing each other, with knees touching. The Summit is behind Cougar to inspire her. They will attempt the first DEEP eye-gaze.

Very few words are spoken; just enough to focus and quiet the mind. DEEP breaths. Feel the energy of Gaia below us. Feel the energy of the Sky Father above us. See the majesty of Shasta and Shastina. Eyes gently open. Keep returning to this space and time when the mind wanders...

Ten minutes in, tears well up in her eyes. Ten minutes later Cougar simply breathes one word at a time...

                    COUGAR (CONT'D)
    Whooo... {inhale} Arree...
    {inhale} Youuu... {searching gaze}

> RACHEL
> I... {inhale} Ammm... {inhale} Lovvve... {eyes wide and clear}

> COUGAR
> Yes!!!

There is so much of a shift in Rachel's understanding and demeanor that Cougar is encouraged to continue these eye-gazes with Heather and other people, men and women, sitting or standing. Each are brought to the verge of tears! The Mountain whispers would guide Cougar each time as what to say for each individual; brief and personally needed insights.

One night, after falling asleep at midnight, Cougar wakes at 3AM. He continues his prayers from earlier in the evening. These are prayers to be of service to those ready to be unblocked of limiting negative energy they habitually hold toward themselves.

The Mountain answers Cougar's prayers and prompts him to visit camp #9. Here in the dead of night! After two minutes struggle, he obeys. He does now also feel a strange calling himself to go there. Someone silently aches. He walks down the familiar trail in the dark, needing no flashlight.

Sometimes they play instruments softly well after midnight but there is no sound coming from the camp this night.

What audacity! He won't drop into any camp after 8PM, let alone a camp with people he has not yet met! He hesitates and turns around, ready to return to bed.

> SHASTA SUMMIT WHISPERS
> Go! This very important for you!
> Do not ignore this calling!

Then Cougar spies a camp fire actively licking the air that encourages him to at least give it a closer look, since he has come this far. As he hikes closer, the more of the camp he can see. Then he realizes no one is around the fire! They must all be in tents, the fire unattended! A lonely table lamp is on as well. He stops, completely discouraged and ashamed of his active imagination.

> COUGAR
> What a fool I am! Who's voice am I really listening to?

> SHASTA SUMMIT WHISPERS
> Are you not up to this turning point transformation? This magical moment will not come again!

Cougar shakes his head and continues bravely onward.

> **COUGAR**
> Oh, well! I am knee DEEP in it now!

Near the entrance of the site, the view opens up. Another world has constructed itself! This cannot be real! At least ten people have materialized out of thin air around the camp fire! And they are all awake! Some are standing but most are sitting quietly in pairs.

> **SHASTINA WHISPERS**
> Be brave! Have Heart! We are with you!

Cougar notes the significance of it being 3:33 in the morning when he reaches the entrance. This emboldens him. Cougar speaks in a low but firm tone:

> **COUGAR**
> I was called here by someone.

The two "guards" standing at the entrance acknowledge him:

> **TWO GUARDIANS**
> Welcome brother.

They signal him to enter. He wanders in and stops at the first pair of young men talking.

> **PEACE**
> When they get angry, you find out this is only because you are mirroring someone else's pain...

Peace continues his instructive monologue as Cougar wonders:

> **COUGAR**
> The group is taken care of with its own guide... Why am I here?

Cougar feels moved to walk around the fire DEEP into the group and to the opposite end of the entrance. He finds an open spot on a blanket and sits down next to a couple who are leaning on each other. He speaks to them:

> **COUGAR (CONT'D)**
> I felt called here by someone.

> **JAMES**
> Thank you for being here.

> **LAURA**
> Who called? You can talk with us.

Peace hears them and stops his conversation. He stands up and bends over the fire menacingly with intensely glaring eyes. In a forceful voice he quizzes them:

>PEACE
>What are you three talking about?

Peace is looking directly at Cougar. If it wasn't quiet enough before, it is now! Cougar looks him straight in the eyes for a long moment. Dead silence. Peace is frozen in his looming position. His menace turns to inquisitiveness.

Finally, quietly and gently, Cougar motions Peace with one hand to come over to him. As if in trance, Peace comes over without a word. Everyone seems to hold their collective breath in suspense. Cougar asks no names this night.

Cougar points for Peace to sit down and guides his knees to touch Cougar's knees. The eye gaze was continuous between them this whole time, even in this half-light.

>COUGAR
>Be still.

Peace visibly calms down.

>COUGAR (CONT'D)
>We are brothers. Be at peace.

He forgets everyone has their eyes glued on him. Cougar has only concern for the afflicted one. Peace watches Cougar transform into an ancient tree. The couple behind him and others see eyes coming out of Cougar in all directions. They are dumbfounded and in awe of a sight never seen before.

This timeless gaze goes on for probably fifteen minutes until Cougar sees tears in Peace's eyes. Everyone is still spellbound. Ten people are alert and in dead silence.

Cougar stands up and places a hand just over Peace's head.

>COUGAR (CONT'D)
>This one is blessed.

Cougar turns and pronounces to the silent group:

>COUGAR (CONT'D)
>You are all blessed beings.

Peace rises, hugs Cougar and turns away. Cougar is satisfied and is exiting around the fire. The two guardians hug Cougar and thank him at the entrance. One then says:

THADDEUS
You probably cannot see me in this dark but I am Thaddeus. We met at Mazi's van. You know, the Persian!

COUGAR
Good to almost see you again! {Pats his back} I remember Mazi's father translates Rumi. How nice!

Cougar leaves for bed as the group talks excitedly about what just took place. Thaddeus stops Peace as he tries to leave.

THADDEUS
How did Cougar know to come to you?

PEACE
Is that his name? I don't know! I was feeling DEEPLY disconnected with our group after all our time together. Cougar somehow knew!

THADDEUS
You were just talking with Jim.

PEACE
Oh, yes! That's it! That was just after finishing up a fire ritual! I was calling in sacred assistance to my dilemma! I was desperate!

PETER
He doesn't know us! How did he know?

JAMES
Who is that Cougar? He has eyes all around him!

JIM
I never met him... but I like him! He is an ancient tree with eyes all around!

The next afternoon, an attractive young woman about thirty years of age is coming down the trail from Upper Panther while Cougar is hiking up from Lower Panther. She locks eyes with him from thirty feet away. He usually looks away until getting closer so that people don't feel too uncomfortable, but something is different this time.

They both keep walking without looking side to side. They don't even look down for inevitable rocks on the trail.

This is one of those impossible scenes right out of Hollywood where two people see nothing else but each other and somehow manage to run toward each other without any kind of careless disaster. The calculated emotional impact of the scene wins the audience over. This spontaneous event that is happening now is even more surreal because this is their first meeting!

She is a wild gypsy woman with intense brown eyes. Her long locks of hair are gracefully wind-blown. They both stop when there is barely two feet between them. With an impish smile some words flow out from her lovely mouth and caress the very air between them.

>LAURA
>I want to go DEEP with you!

Cougar thinks for a moment that he died and went to Sweet Heaven Above. If only he had heard this 36 years ago! He recovers quickly when he remembers his body is 66 years old and more; he is an ancient tree with eyes all over. Those distant pleasures are far behind him. Now Cougar appreciates that beauty simply exists in all its myriad forms. Laura is with serious intent. His response is with no attachments nor the light teasing that he is prone to show. He simply says:

>COUGAR
>Yes!

This response continues the mystery of the trance. Their eyes are still actively engaged... Her boyfriend appears out of nowhere, kisses her on the cheek and leaves.

>JAMES
>See ya' later.

>COUGAR
>{Thinks} Could this be a couple I met in fire-light this morning?

Cougar and Laura continue the gaze for the right amount of time before breaking the trance for the moment.

>COUGAR (CONT'D)
>Let us unblock the trail and go DEEPER into the forest.

>LAURA
>Good! We should not be distracted.

They go up the trail a little and in to the left. They find a good flat spot to sit cross-legged on the Earth with knees touching. Laura prefers the Mountain showing behind Cougar.

They still have not exchanged names. They are only there for the Work. They have mostly silent recognition. They both have healing backgrounds and know how to move energy. Laura hopes Cougar can push her DEEPER beyond her blocks.

The eye gazing lasts about an hour before a long white feather settles between them. A bird chirps contentedly in a tree limb above them. Her karmic edge is open/revealed for her own future probing. She is close, very close.

A couple of days later at site #15, Kokoleka is playing a complex piece he is composing on his Spanish guitar. Amanda is reflecting on the beauty of it. Cougar walks in to listen.

When Kokoleka finishes, he and Amanda tease Cougar for a third day if he wants a Soul reading. Cougar surprisingly accepts this time.

                AMANDA
Cougar! Kokoleka won't do it if you are teasing. You must be serious!

                COUGAR
{Teasing} I will be serious. Watch!

Cougar extends his hand. Kokoleka hesitates.

                KOKOLEKA
Uncle! You are teasing me!

                COUGAR
Not this time. My curiosity wins!

                KOKOLEKA
No "Aum" jokes?

                COUGAR
{Laughing} No "Aum" jokes.

Kokoleka grasps his extended hand but only for a moment. Kokoleka's eyes flutter. He speaks with more intensity.

                ORACLE
You are a human anomaly. Most people have no idea that you have direct access to Everything.

Amanda lies out in the sun close by, still listening.

                ORACLE (CONT'D)
You are an enigma. You are an open book of clarity that people do not see. Only a rare few can utilize what you have to offer to All.

Kokoleka is looking steadily at Cougar.

> ORACLE (CONT'D)
> You are the teachers' Teacher.
> Everyone would be attracted to you
> if they only knew of your Mind
> Treasures; infinite facets of
> crystalline and Universal forms.

The graceful Amanda slips into her tent and then back out again. This does not distract either man from their intent.

> ORACLE (CONT'D)
> Keep your eyes open for a navigator
> who may direct your gifts more
> effectively to others; perhaps a
> charismatic leader who understands
> your Vision, who will multiply your
> energy, working together with you.

Cougar leaves the camp, pondering the truth in this, as the Buddhist Intuitive Drew Daniels spoke of the same things to him in August of 2010 just before Drew passed into THE DEEP.

> SHASTA SUMMIT WHISPERS
> Reach out only to those who are
> Discontent.

> SHASTINA WHISPERS
> Reach out only to those who Hunger.

> CAVE WHISPERS
> Reach out only to those who Seek.

> ETHERIC VOICE
> All else becomes vanity.

Cougar crosses paths with many other talented seekers and continues his energetic eye gazes when directed. He is gifted with mangos, Peruvian bananas, Chinese takeout, walnuts, prayer beads, campfire food, kisses, you name it! What a bountiful year in both directions! No more cave solitude.

Cougar spends much of the last three days on Shasta with four young Argentinians who love to explore. Cougar shows them sacred spots and great views. They show Cougar how they share Malta tea in one hot sipping container. Cougar shares chocolate ginger and almonds. Cico and Thumy make perfect legendary Argentinian campfire Shish Kabobs.

Michelle and Rama take turns sharing Sixties music from the internet. Michelle's face slowly transforms into a young Kathy. Cougar goes back to the dream he had the first night in camp, of Kathy gazing quietly and DEEPLY into his eyes.

PINK FLOYD'S High Hopes from their album Division Bell plays on Michelle's iphone: "In a world of magnets and miracles... Before Time took our dreams away...

"The Light was brighter! With friends surrounded!
The nights of wonder!...

"At a higher altitude with flag unfurled,
we reached the dizzy heights of that dreamed of world!

"With friends surrounded! The Endless River!
Forever and Ever! Forever and Ever!"

INT. COUGAR'S HOUSE - MID-STATE WASHINGTON - 3 JANUARY 2017

Cougar is seen sleeping peacefully in bed. He is lying on his back cross-legged. He just drifted off after a sincere wish to experience the Eternal Love, Luminous Light and Sacred Sound of the Uncreated Creating.

In his dream Cougar hears someone outside the relative safety of his yurt wall. The veil becomes thinner and thinner until we see a face of a human Oracle with emerald-green eyes.

                    COUGAR
        {Bids him} Enter.

The mysterious Oracle pulls open the canvas and enters.

                    ORACLE
        I can see who you are...
        I can show you...

Cougar is now conversing with people he knows and people he doesn't consciously know. They are discussing the hardships of each one's Karmic burdens and lessons on Earth.

Cougar shifts to a "higher" level of less dense Karma with the same people. They are discussing the challenges of Karma that still exist on that level.

They transition up another level and another, discussing the "real" Karma of each level until they reach a level of no Karma at all! They are free of Karma. They are free of form. No bodies. They are free of Mind. No thoughts.

We are Wisdom beyond Knowledge. We are Everything. We touch Everything! We are Collective Living Gnosis and beyond. We are all reporting back from our places and positions until there are no places and positions.

Cougar sees that everyone is simultaneously on all these levels NOW, just not consciously from the human perspective.

Cougar is travelling to where we are all Masters, Immense Buddhas and Bodhisattvas right NOW. Cougar is travelling even beyond the level of Masters, Buddhas and Bodhisattvas who are living in 3D bodies right now.

We have no names, no separation by any title. We are all equal sparks of God, stardust of the Uncreated Creating.

Cougar discovers that he is travelling without travelling. He is reaching without seeking. This is so beyond language that anything said now about it is twisted by the Mind.

Levels? Dimensions? Simultaneous Dimensions? Parallel lives? Soul Travel? Planes of Existence? 3D? Real? Unreal? Dreams? These are all useless terms here in THIS Spaciousness!

We are so Dynamic! We are so Eternal! What made this so? Who are we? What Being or Beings or non-Beings made this come about? Who are we reporting to? Why do we need to painfully grow on Earth if we came from Everything? Where does Divine Compassionate Love come from? We are Love too! How is this Love covered in so many layers of mud until we lose Love?

We only begin to discover the "True" answers to this level of inquiry when we are stable in THIS space.

Cougar is blessed and graced to enter this Spaciousness this day. Not just the blue sky of Peace. Not just the clear blue sky of Stillness, but the dynamically Luminous Blue Sky! He knew everything without trying to know. All comes at a whim of curiosity. Nothing is withheld from us. Total Freedom!

That Luminosity goes far beyond sight into the vast Infinite. Emptiness? Fullness? Void? Ha! Poorly crafted words for the Wordless! Cougar got a little taste, only to lose much of it.

The mortal coil entangles Cougar once again. He is slowly compressing back into the dense body. He sees from the inside that the Light is leaving through the Crown of the head. He tries to absorb some of this Light into his eager cells.

100,000 x 100,000 bubbles of All-Seeing Eyes of Light slowly continue their escape plan. Cougar is left vibrating and trembling for 45 minutes in the darkness of his room.

EXT. NATIONAL FOREST - CA? CO? WA? - 1974 FUTURE VISION 2034

Fifteen people are engaged in the Drum Dance. Three people are on the Grand-Father Drum. Clouds start moving in. Tom is one of the three on the drum. He signals Lorraine over.

                TOM WING
Lorraine, the drum cannot get wet.

Lorraine shakes her head in agreement.

> TOM WING (CONT'D)
> See if we need to stop the dance.

Lorraine dances over to Cougar and whispers in his ear. Cougar nods and signals Mike to come with him. Mike and Cougar walk away from the dance and into the sparse trees.

> COUGAR
> Mike, I've been thinking about how Darkness needs us, not to destroy it but to return it to the Light...

Mike's eyes grow wide and he points:

> MIKE
> Look, Cougar, here comes the rain! We should stop the dance and cover the drum. We only have a few moments.

Cougar walks a little further as the rain approaches. Cougar holds out his hands. As he stops walking, the wall of rain stops just a few feet before him.

> COUGAR
> The drum is protected. Tell Tom to continue.

Mike shrugs his shoulders, giving way to an old unspoken trust between them. Sighing...

> MIKE
> The impossible is on you again!

Mike turns around to walk back to the Dance. Cougar turns his head back toward Mike.

> COUGAR
> Mike!

> MIKE
> {Stops and turns facing Cougar}
> Yes?

> COUGAR
> Buds forever!

> MIKE
> Buds forever!

Mike continues walking back to the dance.

                    COUGAR
          {Lowering voice} Mankind is
          destined for Great Things yet...
          Gladly, with my life, I will see
          this through to the End.

Cougar takes another step or two forward and reaches a hand
into the wall of rain. He brings his wet hand back to his
mouth and touches two of those fingers to his lips.

                    COUGAR (CONT'D)
          The tears of the Angels guide us.

Mike walks back to Tom. Tom shakes his head in disbelief but
continues to drum. Cougar walks back into the Dance Circle
with his eyes toward the sky. The sky stays clear above the
Dance.

Everyone can see the wall of rain but they continue to dance
as if their lives depend on it. Cougar laughs a little as his
eyes stay focussed upward.

Seven dancers in the Outer Circle have mud caked on their
faces from an earlier Mud Man ritual. One at a time they link
together, hands on the shoulders of the one in front of each
of them until all Seven are dancing that way together.

Cougar holds his hands up in the air, palms up. He laughs
again.

A silver saucer floats into the blue sky space above the
Dance and hovers. Is this a manifestation of the Uncreated
Creating?... A lens-portal to another dimension/Density?

An intensely white beam descends on Cougar and he lights up.
Glowing radiantly, he is transformed into a pure light being
and is quickly pulled up into the Heavenly Orb as rainbow
light. The great light fades out. Many of the dancers have
seen this but the drummers keep drumming and the dancers keep
dancing.

The Seven Mud Men begin to wail and hold a hand up to the
blue sky which is in stark contrast to the misty grey mass
circling around them.

The rain breaks its wall and sweeps into the Dance Circle.
The Drum is mysteriously protected.

The rain washes the mud off from the Seven Faces to expose
glowing light and happiness. They look like Seven Beings of
Light.

The rain passes away quickly, showing the other dancers are
dazed yet joyous from the contagion of the Seven uplifted.

ENDE

"How could any Human dare to break the idols or steer the craft that Gods and Goddesses use?"   Tablet 10

"The bigger part of Him was made in Heaven and the smaller part somewhere on Earth... He knew the secret paths that reached the eagles' nest above the mountain."   Tablet 1

"Who shall descend to Hell and redeem the drum from where it rests unused? {"Anahata" is Sanskrit for the unstruck drum of the Heart.}   ...Who shall risk his life to retrieve the precious gifts of Inanna from Death?"   Tablet 12

"Utnapishtim, allow Him to wear the sacred Elder's cloak, a cloak unstained and Unstainable."   Tablet 11

Gilgamesh   2600 BC

This is the earliest discovered Hero's Journey to date. Famous text for cursing the Goddess, destroying the Bull of Heaven {the Age of Taurus} that protected her and bringing in the Age of Aries, Patriarchy.

With this text, our 21st Century Leonian Hero, born in the Tibetan year of the Tiger, honors and restores the value of the Feminine at the Dawning of the Age of Aquarius.

The Age of Pisces is fading away, but not without a struggle.

All Ages rise and fall to the Eons of Time.

Love, Light & Sound.
Power, Wisdom & Compassion.
Virtue, Gratitude & Immortality.
That is all one needs to know!
All else falls into place,
in perfect Harmony.
Cougar3

www.ingramcontent.com/pod-product-compliance
Lightning Source LLC
LaVergne TN
LVHW021816060526
838201LV00058B/3406